Social Intelligence

A prerequisite for Law Enforcement Professionals, (Sworn and Civilian)

Author:

Michael A. Gray M.A.Ed.

Motivationer Speaker

Educator/Trainer

The biggest obstacle to learning something new is the belief that you already know it

Intelligence refers to being intelligent about our social life: more socially conscious, better able to handle disturbing situations, more sensitive to the emotions of others and able to put all that together to create effective, nursing interactions. Some police officers I'll better than others at these fundamental human skills, the the good news is all of these abilities can be learned. In any domain of humanity, when it comes to cultivating expertise it helps to have guidelines from extras themselves. As an know saying saying puts it, if you want to get to the top of the mountain, as someone who goes up and down the path to the summit.

The Law Enforcement Officers' Bill of Rights

Though the law enforcement officers' bill of rights varies from state to state, the most common provisions include:

- Officers should be informed of any pending investigations against them, unless informing them would compromise the integrity of the case

- Officers should be informed of the outcome of the investigation and of any recommendations made regarding discipline

- Interviews should be conducted while the officer is on duty whenever practical or possible

- Officers should be informed of the name, rank and command of the officer overseeing the investigation

- Officers should be permitted to have an attorney or representative present with them during any interrogation

- Officers must not be threatened or promised rewards in exchange for their testimony

- Officers should be entitled to a hearing regarding the final disposition of the investigation, with access to the allegations and evidence presented against them

- Officers should have the opportunity to provide written commentary and attach it to any adverse information, such as complaints and disciplinary action that is placed in their personnel files.

- Officers should not be subject to retaliation for exercising these rights

Get the results you're looking for!

1. Bring our powerful, high-impact workbook to your organization and show your employees you're serious about their professional growth and achieving critical organizational goals and objectives.

Maximizer your training budget!

2. Our ethic workbook allows you to train work groups, teams and entire departments for less than the cost of traditional public seminars or other training options.

3. Give your staff the skills, knowledge and confidence they need to meet tough workplace challenges head-on, realize their full potential and perform at their peak.

Guaranteed Results!

All of our workbooks are **100% satisfaction guaranteed!** We're confident this workbook will provide you with the tips and techniques you need to stay calm and productive in any situation. If for any reason you are dissatisfied, sent us a letter (Attn: customer relations) within 30 days of your purchase stating the reason you were not satisfied, and we will arrange for you to return the book -hassle free.

For more consultation, email or call us at

Michael. Gray @ymail.com

916-494-3498

Michael Gray M.A.Ed

Social intelligence for the law-enforcement professional is the sole property Michael Gray.

All rights reserved. No part of this book may be reproduced or transmitted in any form or by any means electronic or mechanical, including photographing, recording are by any informational storage and retrieval system without permission in writing from Michael Gray.

Social Intelligence: **Independent Workbook**

The 4 core components of this training are

- The role of professional and customer service in law enforcement

- The importance of emotional intelligence and its relationship to customer service within the law enforcement community

- Active listening during service and effective communication of officers

- Elements of effective law enforcement leadership practices

Social Intelligence

Pre-Assignment

Complete this worksheet before the class begins. Makes note of what you hope to learn or goals you want to address after the class.

1) In your own words, what is social intelligence? Have you ever heard this term before?
   _____
   _____
   _____

2) Why is social intelligence important at home and work?
   _____
   _____
   _____

3) What areas of social intelligence would you be more interested in learning about?
   _____
   _____
   _____

4) What do you hope to learn or take away from this class?
   _____
   _____
   _____

Any other thoughts:
_____
_____
_____
_____
_____
_____

Introduction

Happened to Officer friendly ?

Law enforcement in a free society must strike a delicate balance between protecting individual rights to professional service especially from government-sponsored agencies and the society's interest in professional ethical decision-making by law enforcement professionals. Often this is seen as one between a principal defense of civil rights and a mere Unitarian interest in improving the continuity of customer service. There is no certain place to fix the line between appropriate and Impermissible police and law enforcement professional conduct. What is most conspicuous about this area of ethics and customer service in law enforcement is the lack of controlling standards for defining the roles of law enforcement officers and law enforcement professionals. The purpose of the Law Enforcement Leadership and Ethics Training is to prevent breaches of the peace; enforce the laws, directives and regulations which govern the law enforcement agencies and to protect its employees, the facilities, its assets and the nation's currency" which function in synchronization. Trainees will be able to consult a menu of techniques and be encouraged to contribute ideas of their own.

One weakness of many pre-packaged development trainings is their reliance on a single, generic approach. The standard training program, where everyone goes through a cookie-cutter experience, turns out to have the worst return on investment. This training gives people the power to tailor their own learning plans to their own aspirations, by using self-directed learning that place control of the change process in the hands of students. After all, they're in control anyway. This approach merely avoids the delusion of facility control.

Section I

The Role of Professional and Customer Service in Law Enforcement

Social Intelligence for the Law enforcement professional

Take this little survey

(It's a real eye-opener)

Let's face it; most of us already understand how we should act in certain situations-: Cool in a crisis, positive when things go wrong, emotionally consistent with our loved ones, persistent when breaking a bad habit are taking on a new, constructive one.

Yet, why is it so hard for us to do what we know is best?

It isn't. Not if you use the principles you'll gain in this training.

Think about it-how much do you know about the topics listed below? And how much of that knowledge do you put to use in your life? Let's find out.

Circle the number that measures your knowledge about a subject. Then, put an" X" through the number that measures your actual performance.

(1 Being low, 10 High)

Motivating people

1   2   3   4   5   6   7   8   9   10

Handling crisis

1   2   3   4   5   6   7   8   9   10

Weight control

1   2   3   4   5   6   7   8   9   10

Time management

1   2   3   4   5   6   7   8   9   10

Dealing with stress

1   2   3   4   5   6   7   8   9   10

Managing conflict

1   2   3   4   5   6   7   8   9   10

Being your best

What does the best mean to you? These three simple words, put together, have a profound meaning, a meaning that can change your life, totally and completely. Before you do anything, think these three words. Recite them to yourself. Make them your credo. And live by them. Whatever you do, give it your all, exceed your own expectations, surpass what you did yesterday, do everything with quality, think accelerants. Always being your best.

Man who holds the key to his own prison we'll soon be persuaded to fit it into the lock.

Handout 10-1

Leadership and Customer Service

The Forum Corporation, in its "Customer Focus Research" project (1988), identified

Leadership factors that set customer-focused companies apart. This research concludes that

Managers set the tone for the outcome of delivering excellent customer service—what we

Call "Fantastic Service Every Time". As a leader, you are the model for your staff.

The following actions can enhance the public service climate in your sector.

Public **Service**

1. Setting public service performance goals and standards

- Talk about what putting the public first means to you and to the

Department.

- Communicate clear goals and standards that support professional service.
- Communicate what you expect your officers and civil-service staff to do when dealing with the public.
- Develop public service goals and standards for performance reviews.

2. Providing leadership that help solve complaintent ' problems. When there is a problem when the complainant receives a citation, listen to the customer side of the story.

- Let the customer know that you appreciate their comments
- Explain your decision and why you made it.

- Decide together how a similar situation might be handled the next time it occurs.

- Make an effort to help remove obstacles that hinder customers understanding.

- Set a personal example of good customer service, using excellent communication

    Skills.

3. Finding better ways to earn public trust.

- Ask employees who have contact with the public for information on customer

Needs or expectations.

- Seek opportunities to try new ways of doing things to serve the public better, don't be so quick to draw your at the first sign of an argument.

- Ask and consider other officers' ideas about improving the quality of public service.

4. Helping officers enhance their public relations.

- Give honest and direct feedback about how well your officers are serving the public.

Continued on next page

Handout 10-1, continued

Leadership and Customer Service

- Help officers learn from positive and negative experiences when dealing with the public.

- Be sensitive to the "contact overload" syndrome and provide ways for officers to relieve stress.

- Observe officers' communication skills to see if they are in the right role.

The Internal Environment

1. Using the systems approach to serve the public

   - Identify policies and procedures that interfere with serving the public well, and change methods to achieve better public service.

   - Provide the support and resources that are needed to serve the public well.

   - Use the departments marketing or public research to improve service.

   - When asked, always help staff with customer problems.

   - Provide civil service workers with the resources they need to serve the public.

   - Insist on cooperation rather than competition within the department, and model cooperative behavior.

   - Keep all staff informed about the public's needs and expectations.

2. Increasing the ability to serve the public

- Cross-that will service workers to maximize use of talents and encourage workers to assist other departments.

- Encourage officers and civil service workers to feel that being responsive to the public needs is their personal responsibility and not someone else's job.

   - Function as a team in serving the public.

- Ensure that customer relations skills are an important factor in deciding who is hired to work with the public.
- Reward sworn officers and civil-service workers for doing a good job of serving the public.

3. Valuing excellence
    - Resolve customers' problems to their satisfaction.
    - Personally provide high-quality service to the public.

4. Relating with the public
    - Regularly ask customers about their needs or expectations.
    - Regularly collect feedback from customers about the quality of the service received.
    - Employ a "whatever it takes" policy to remedy the situation for a dissatisfied customer.
    - Use information about the needs or expectations of the public to identify ways to serve them better.

Handout 10-2

Motivating Team Members

Each person on your team is unique. Motivating sworn officers and civil-service workers with different personalities and different needs are not easy, but it can be challenging and rewarding.

Increasing Motivation

Achievement and recognition are strong motivators. Here are some ways those supervisors can help increase the harmony of sworn officers and civil-service workers:

- Recognize achievement when you see it.
- Recognize steps toward reaching a goal; don't always wait for the end product or Total behavior change.
- Brainstorm a list of ways you can show appreciation. Include some ways that would be a stretch for you—things you would not think about doing.
- On a weekly basis, record at least one achievement that has been accomplished by each one of your staff members.

Note whether you recognized the achievement. Then do as suggested above to notice and recognize more achievement.

Praise

When asked what type of recognition people want, the answer is often, "I just wish my Boss would say 'hello.'" How often that comes up; how simple it seems. Here are a number of other ways to recognize employees:

Continued on next page

Motivation factors help employees do a better job and improve productivity. Theorists suggest that the four strongest motivation Factors are:

1. Achievement: Feeling personal accomplishment for having done a job well

2. Recognition: Being recognized for doing your job well; for example, being complimented by your boss or receiving an award

3. Participation: Being personally involved in your work; taking responsibility for decisions you have made.

4. Growth: Having the opportunity to be challenge by your job, such as the chance to learn skills and knowledge.

Handout 10-2, continued

Motivating officers and civil-service workers

- Give thank-you cards at work.
- Send thank-you cards to officers and civil service workers' homes.
- Present "job well done" cards.
- Tell officers and civil-service workers how good you feel about what they did and how it helps the department.
    - Take a staff member out to lunch or dinner as a reward for a specific project.
- Organize events and activities, or lead an employee activities committee that includes both sworn officers and civil service workers.
    - Give specific praise in front of others.
- Arrange for officers and civil-service workers to have lunch or breakfast with the head of the department.

- Give time off.
- Delegate. (This is a reward to many officers and so service workers because it shows your faith

And trust.)

- Work on the front line with your department staff.
- Hold informative meetings about the department.
- Offer professional workshops and fun workshops.
- Frame and display positive letters from the public.
- Do a cheer with your department one morning.
- Create a department song with staff members. Videotape the production.
- Take some time to walk around during the day to observe your area.
- Have informal discussions with your department during your walks.

Handout 13-5

The Fantastic Public Service Equation

Equotation Components

1. Greeting the public
2. Determining needs
3. Meeting needs
4. Making the movement memorable
5. Checking results
6. Leaving the door open

Component 1. Greeting the public. Responsive service starts with the response in greeting. You only get one first chance to impress a customer, and their first chance lasts only a matter of seconds. The public suspected friendly greeting, complete with eye contact, smile, and receptive body language. It's basic: a greeting recognizes a person words right from the start and established rapport. A proper greeting immediately says, I'm here to serve," which is what public worship was imprisoned service is all about.

Component 2. Determining needs, finding out what the public need determines the rest of the interactions. Listening and asking questions is fundamental to this part of the importation. Listening provided us the opportunity to help with understanding the needs of the public, the public concerns and with solving problems. Where active listening is a key ingredient in providing responsive, empathetic service. When you listen, give the customer your undivided attention and respect. Proactive listening involves total concentration, paraphrasing, and understanding their feelings allowing us to work together with the customer for their benefit.

Component 3. Meeting the public's needs. When needs are determined, it is time to act. Responding effectively includes acting quickly and with confidence. It requires finding out information, being available to ask questions and guiding the customer toward a solution.

Component 4. Making the movement memorable. This is where you do something special. It could be something big or something little. Creating a memorable moment could be as simple as walking the customer to his or her designation rather than pointing are telling her where to go.

There are many great stories of memorable moments. Consider this one: Nordstrom's, a department store that is well known for outstanding service, once had a disgruntled customer come in with a defective tire. The store gladly took the tire back, and refunded the customer's money. What's so unusual about this story? Nordstrom's doesn't sell tires.

Component 5. Check your results. There is an easy way to see of your department is giving fantastic service. Companies and organizations spend a lot of money on surveys, and other means of soliciting customer's feedback. The front-line officers and civil-service workers can be the first to give feedback simply by asking, "How was our service today?" Even asking with sincerity, "is there anything else we can do for you?" Is a way to see of all the public needs have been met.

You can promote other services when you check results. You can offer the option of another services, are you can tell a customer something he didn't know about your department. Departments Checking results help solidify the relationship with the public and improve the image in the public eyes.

The public's reply may not always be positive. We asked for their opinions, the public may complain. A complaint, however, is just an opportunity. It points you towards things to make better and ways to improve. Handling a complaint can be a memorable moment.

Key point: a complaint is a memorable moment waiting to happen. Research shows that when a person complain and get their complaints solved satisfactorily are actually more loyal than if they had no problem at all.

By involving the public in your department asked them about their opinions you pave the way for public loyalty. Seek

Component 6. Leaving the door open. There are many ways to encourage the public to praise your department. The public like to be appreciated. Leaving the door open is a way to say, **"Please come back,"** or" **Thanks for your support."** It is a way to recognize them and support to patronage.

- Thanks for your support."
- Hope you come back to buy your next policeman ball tickets."
- Call me personally if you have any more questions."
- I'll be looking forward to seeing you at the policeman ball.

What Do Sworn Officers and Civil-Service Workers Do That Makes the Public Angry?

The public become upset for a number of reasons, many of which don't have much to do with the police or customer service your department provides. These include:

Unmet expectations: This could be related to how the public expected to be treated or how they think police protective services should be provided.

Untrained personnel: People really don't want to be the test subject for a trainee. They want their problems to be handled by people who know what to do.

This side of the organization: People who have had previous bad experiences with the department are had heard negative things about the department may react more angrily when something goes wrong than they would otherwise.

Is the only way: Some customers think the only way they can get their needs met is to be angry and demand better service.

Discourtesy: Naturally, people are angry when they feel they have been treated without respect.

Ignored: people who feel they are being ignored or, such as those whose phone calls are not return, react angrily.

Conflicting stories: When people are told one thing by one civil-service worker and something else by another, they naturally become angry, because it appears that someone is lying to them.

Argument: if someone in the department has argued with the customer, the customer will often have to be handled carefully in order to return them to a state of calmness.

Feelings invalidated: When you tell someone they shouldn't feel a certain way, it often angers them, because it implies that their feelings are unimportant or wrong.

Previous state: if a customer is already upset, tired, or under stress when he comes in, it is easy for him to be upset.

Frustration: If the customer is having difficulty getting help, he can easily become angry. For example, a customer who is transferred from department to department may lose his temper, particularly if he feels helpless.

Honesty is challenged: A customer who feels that his integrity is being question will often react with anger.

Embarrassment: People are angry when they are embarrassed, and they often lash out unfairly.

Vindication: Some people are determined to prove themselves right, whether it is really necessary or not.

Failure to listen: To those who feel as if they are not given a chance to tell their side of the story often react extremely negatively.

Personality: Some customers are just naturally contrary, and they don't need much of an excuse to fly off the handle.

Personal prejudice: Everyone has prejudice, and some people are unable to control them. The person may be prejudiced against your skin color, your department, your cologne; while virtually anything else conceivable.

Manipulation: Some customers may use anger as a method of intentionally manipulating others.

How to Keep a Handle on Your Own Emotions

There are things you can do to prevent yourself from overreacting to difficult people while still managing the interaction effectively. They include:

If things get overly intense, take a break from the situation, even if it is only for a few minutes. Excuse yourself in a polite manner, and be sure to give the customer a legitimate reason for leaving.

If the person is making unreasonable demands, try read phrasing and repeating yourself. For instance, if the person insists on immediate answer but your supervisor will not be in until the next day, you may use the statements: my supervisor won't be in until tomorrow. I'm sorry; he's already gone for the day. I'll see to it that he calls you first thing in the morning. Eventually, if you remain calm, the massage is likely to get through, particularly if your behaviors show your sincerity.

If you have tried to solve the problem and can't seem to satisfy the person, ask him what you can do to make him happy.

Be alert for potential violence. Look for the following nonverbal cues that potentially violent people often display:

- clenched fist
- enraged facial expressions
- flared nostrils
- a tense body
- flushed skin tones
- leaning forward
- shouting
- angry, tense voice tones
- If you feel threatened, call for assistance immediately. No risk-taking
- Assert yourself when it is productive to do so and avoid doing so if it is not.
- Learn to laugh at yourself.

- Don't succumb to anger.
- Take responsibility for your emotions.
- Don't try to reason with a person's who seems to be on alcohol or other drugs, and don't accuse anyone of drinking and taking drugs.
- Don't keep thinking about the things that made you angry.
- Maintain a positive self-esteem.
- Learn to treat others as equals, and give them the benefit of the doubt.
- Don't try to control others.

10/5 rule

Another powerful behavior you can adopt is the 10/5 rule. It's something that has existed in the hospitality industry since the beginning of time, and yet it's surprising that it is not used more fully in police departments.

Whenever you pass someone (coworker or customer) within 10 feet of you, it is your responsibility to give this person eye contact and a smile. If you pass within 5 feet of someone, then you offer a personal greeting.

This should be a culture behavior in your department. When one embraces an attitude of service, it's lived 360°, and without boundaries as to whether it's internal or external.

Assessment 12 – 3   Fantastic Public Service Every Time Survey

Determining Needs

- Continue:

- Improving:

Meeting Needs

- Continue:

- improve:

Making the moment memorable

- Continue:

- improve:

Checking Results

- continue:

- improved:

Leaving the door open

- continue:

- improve:

Connecting sworn officers and civil services workers to the mission appreciated inquiry

Appreciated inquiry is a team-based management technique that focuses on sworn officers and civil service workers stress. Employees identify departmental processes that work well, envision processes that work well in the future, plan and prioritize processes that work well, and implement the proposals. A key task of ethical leadership is aligning employee strengths so that employee weaknesses are relevant.

Appreciation of inquiry is a particularly powerful method for aligning fence sitters and adversarial employees, as well as go-getters, with continuous improvement efforts and superior performance. The heart of an organization's mission is to serve customers. An appreciation of inquiry workshop where superior customer service can be designed around the following steps:

Step 1: Individually reflect on superior public service. Employee independently response to the following prompts:

- Describe a situation where you receive superior public service.
- Describe a situation where you provide a superior public service.
- Describe a situation when a coworker provided superior public service.
- Describe other ways the department has provided superior public service.
- Describe other ways the department can provide superior public service.
- What changes would have to be made in the department to achieve this?

Step 2: In a small team, determined the essential elements of superior public service. Each team member present situations where he or she receive superior public service, provided public superior public service, and observe others in the organizations providing superior service. As a team, lives the important elements mentioned in these stories that enable employees to achieve superior public service (e.g. "the common themes in this story are X and Y.") Share these elements with the larger group.

Step 3: Develop a collective vision of what is needed to achieve superior public service. Each team member describes other ways the department can provide superior public service and changes that would have to be made to accomplish this. For instance, "we could improvise a superior public service if we did x and y." As a team, develop a compelling image of how the department can achieve superior public service in the future. Share this image with a larger group.

Step 4: Create a draft of a new departmental mission statement that emphasizes superior public service at every level up of operations. Each team member independently composes a one second mission statement and presents it to the team. As a team, achieve consensus on a one second mission statement that meets the following four criteria, sure the mission statement with the larger group:

1. Is it desired? Would they want it?

2. Must be stated in affirmative and bold terms.

3. Is the go clear and reachable?

4. Does it stretch and challenge the organization in a desired direction?

Step 5: Determine the department's current "positive core." Each team member independently determines three core aspects of the department that already support superior public service. For each aspect, provide examples. For instance," we're already good at doing X and Y." as a team, reach consensus on the core aspects. Share the core aspects, and examples, with the larger group.

Step 6: Make personal commitments. Each team member independently list what he or she would do more of, are differently, to deliver superior customer service. For instance, "I promise to do X and Y." Share this information with team members and hold each other accountable. Share these commitments with the larger group.

Step 7: Make departmental action recommendations. Each team member recommends initiatives for how the department can achieve superior public service. How can the vision and image (step 3), mission statement (step 4), current strengths (step 5), and personal commitments (step 6), become a highly integrated reality? As a team, develop these recommendations they shared with the larger group.

Step 8: Have shift supervisor's follow-up. As an example of superior public service and accountability, supervisors commit to providing feedback on this information within a reasonable timeframe.

Section II

The importance of emotional intelligence, and its relationship to customer service within the law enforcement community

This emotional intelligence section was written to help civil service employees and sworn law enforcement officers become more attuned to their inter-signals, recognizing how their feelings affect them and their job performance. They will become attuned to their guiding values and can often intuit the best course of action, and seeing the big picture in a complex situation. Emotionally self-aware sworn officers and civic workers can be candid and authentic, able to speak openly about their emotions and are aware of their conviction about their guiding wisdom.

Emotional intelligence can help sworn officers and civil service workers with high self-awareness, typically know their limitations and strengths, and exhibit a sense of humor about them-selves. They examine a gracefulness in learning where they need to improve, and welcome constructive criticism and feedback.

Emotional intelligence also helps officers and civil service workers with empathy that allows them to attune to a wide range of emotional signals. During this course officers and civil service workers will learn to listen attentively and grasp the other person's perspective. Empathy makes sworn officers, and civil services workers able to get along well with people of diverse backgrounds are from other cultures.

Are you emotionally literate?

Emotional intelligence is not merely about controlling emotional responses for one's own benefit and that of others. It is also about using emotions when and where suitable. Emotion is, after all, at the heart of that sincerity which reassures, persuades and affords confidence; emotions triggers flight of fight, sometimes appropriate; emotion is necessary if we are to cope, for example, with Bereavement; emotion collide at the source of our greatest joys. Emotional intelligent are like parents to their emotions, acknowledging their needs, loving them, indulging them were appropriate, encouraging their creativity yet restraining them from full destructive are discarded behavior. To extend the metaphor, the emotionally intelligent are neither "seen but not heard," nor of one which would allow the little darlings to "express themselves" freely to the discomfort our dismay of others. Emotional literacy with regard to others can only be learned by reference to the ABC awards own emotions. If, therefore, you are not at ease with your own emotions, you will find it hard to relate to others and to respond appropriately to them.

Circle the answers that come closest to your own emotional response;

1. Your child, in direct contravention to your orders, runs into the busy road. You pull him/her back and:

   a) Smack or shake him or her?

   b) Message your emotions and explain why this was not a good idea?

   c) Message your emotions and resolve upon subsequent punishment?

2. You then:

   a) Yell at the child and threaten him/her with dire punishment?

   b) Apologize and explain that mommy/daddy was frightened?

   c) Burst into tears?

3. It annoys you to:

   a) Not knowing how to make the most of your physical attributes at work?

b) See others making the most of their physical attributes at work?

c) See others unkempt or sloppy dress at work?

4. You are infuriated with your partner. Do you:
a) Refuse to speak for days?
b) Skip work, and go for a walk?
c) Pilot revisions?

5. Your parent/parent-in-law is nagging, sarcastic and interfering. Your principal feeling is:
a) Resentment?
b) Resignation?
c) Pity?

6. Grief is:
a) A necessary and salutary process?
b) Such a waste, in time all will heal?
c) A blemish on your life?

7. Does worry serve a purpose?
a) Sometimes?
b) Never?
c) Always?

8. You are outraged by a newspaper story. Do you:
a) Rant after friends/family?
b) Write a letter to the newspaper?

c) Become depressed?

9. Is your anger:

a) A spur to change?

b) A spur to hurt are destroyed things?

c) Destructive of yourself?

10. Time is, above all:

a) The great healer?

b) The great destroyer?

c) To be ignored our vanquished?

11. A violent crime is, to you

a) "A reflection of a general trend in society?"

b) "An isolated, tragic case for which we can draw a lesson?"

c) "An outraged about which something should be done?"

12. You like music to be, primarily:

a) Soothing?

b) Exciting?

c) Deeply moving?

Are you emotionally literate?

1. A.) 3, _____	b)2,	c)1
2. A)3, c)1_____	b)2,	
3. A)2 _____	b)1	c)3
4. A)1 c)2_____	b)3	
5. A)2, _____	b)1,	c)3
6. A)3, _____	b)1,	c)2
7. A)3, _____	b)1,	c)2
8. A)2, c)1_____	b)3	
9. A)3, _____	b)2,	c)1
10. A)3, _____	b)1,	c)2
11. A)1, _____	b)3,	c)2
12. A)1, _____	b)2,	c)3

12-19: You are ill at ease with your emotions, and thus, for all your apparent good intentions, you take refuge in "appropriate" response, often of bland submissiveness. You cannot confront your emotions honestly, acknowledging that they are, however violent, valid, you can only repress them or simulate a proper response rather than turning them to constructive use. Remember that all emotions have been felt before and are, to greater or lesser extent, common to all humans.

20-27: Your robust attempts to master your emotions are praiseworthy but frequently ill, judged and unsympathetic. You defend yourself from unworthy emotions by simulating appropriate responses, but you tend to give rent-free space in your head to people and things which were better considered, understood and cosigned to the emotional databank for subsequent use. Try allowing emotions, even emotions with same unworthy-anger, fear, frailty, depression, and etc.-Into harmless contexts such as when listening to music or watching films, explore them and acknowledge them. They are part of the armory wisdom.

28-36 you have no problem in accepting and using your emotions when appropriate, while imposing restraint on destructive impulses. You are comfortable with your natural responses where they served their turn and know how to channel their useful psychological consequences to best effect.

Developing your Social intelligence

This instrument, "developing your social intelligence," is designed to help you gain awareness of your abilities in terms of social intelligence and then to help you develop these abilities.

The instrument consists of three parts

Part one requires you to rate your ability to apply social intelligence.

Part two requires you to examine your response as important one, looking for strengths and for areas that can be improved.

Part three requires you to practice and observe your skills in applying emotional intelligence for four weeks. Then you retake parts one and two, noting differences from your earlier responses.

For each item, rate how well you are able to display the ability described. Before responding, trying to think of actual situations in which you have been called on to use the ability.

Low ability   **High ability**

1   2   3   4   5   6   7

1. Identify changes in conscious arousal   _____

3. Act productively when angry   _____

4. Act productively in situations that aroused anxiety   _____

5. Calm yourself quickly when angry   _____

6. Associate different psychological cues with different emotions   _____

7. Use self "talk" to affect your emotional states   _____

8. Communicate your feelings effectively   _____

9. Reflect on negative feelings without reason   _____

10. Stay calm when you are negatively the targeted by others   _____

11. Know when you are thinking negatively   _____

12. Know when your-self talk is or isn't helping you _____

13. Know when you are getting angry _____

14. Know how to manage events you encounter _____

15. Know what six senses you are currently using _____

16. Accurately communicate about your experience _____

17. Identify what information influences your understanding _____

18. Identify your mood shifts _____

19. Know when you you're becoming defensive _____

20. Know the impact that your anger has on others _____

21. Know when you communication breaks down _____

22. Can see when others are physically angry _____

23. Regroup quickly after being upset _____

24. Complete long-term tasks _____

25. Perform well when doing uninteresting work _____

26. Change ineffective habits _____

27. Develop more productive behavior _____

28. Follow words with actions _____

29. Resolve your own conflicts peacefully _____

30. Develop understanding with others _____

31. Help resolve conflict between others _____

32. Exhibit effective communication skills _____

33. Articulate the faults of yourself _____

34. Influence others, directly or indirectly _____

35. Build trust with groups different than yours _____

36. Develop support teams _____

37. Make others feel confidence in them _____

38. Provide support to others, as needed _____

39. Accurately reflect feelings back to others _____

40. Recognize when another person is in pain _____

41. Help others manage their emotions _____

42. Show empathy to others even if you don't like that person _____

43. Engaged in intimate conversations with others _____

44. Help a group to manage emotions _____

45. Detect indifference between others emotions or feelings _____

Review your responses. The following charts indicate which items reflect which competencies.

Intrapersonal

Self-awareness	Managing emotions	Self-motivation
1,6,11,12,13,14 15,17,18,19,20,21	1,2,3,4,5,7,9,10 13,27	7,22,23,25,26, 27,28

Interpersonal

Relating well	emotional mentoring
8,10,16,19,20,29 30,31,32,33,34,35 36,37,38,39,42,43 44,45	8,10,16,18,34,35 37,38,39,40,41, 44,45

Organize your responses as follows. For each of the five competencies, count the number responses for which you score for lower using check marks in the left column. Complete number responses for which you score 5 or higher using check marks in the right column.

Intrapersonal

Competency	Response of 4 and lower	Responses of 5 and higher
Self-awareness		
Managing emotions		
Self-motivation		

Interpersonal

Competency	responses of 4 and lower	responses of 5 and higher

Relating well

Emotional mentoring

Study your patterns and identify which competencies you want to improve.

Part three

Based on your response pattern, identified to emotional intelligent competencies that you wish to focus on improving:

1._____

2._____

Now identify some specific tasks that will help you master these two competencies of emotional intelligence:

During the next four weeks, practice using your emotional intelligence abilities.

Then retake parts one and two. No differences. Repeat the procedures until your response is five or above or all of the items in part one.

Self-control

Self-control requires that we master our emotions. This mastery enables us to understand both positive and negative emotions in a way that enables us to learn from our emotions rather than be burdened by them. We can anticipate and use our emotional reactions that are most often associated with a person who lacks self-control, but emotional self-control is more than just controlling our anger. Self-control also means finding productive ways to address self-doubt. Self-control requires us to know how to express emotions appropriately-both positive emotions and negative emotions.

Positive self-control required that we know when to express emotions that will get us the results were looking for. Emotions must be express authentically. Turning up the volume on positive emotions such as pride our gratitude does it mean being something that you're not? Self-control simply means finding ways to express emotions appropriately. I mean appropriate to you and to the outcome that you intended.

I often think about emotional climate in terms of a music metaphor, subliminal music that plays in the background. That music deals clues to the emotional climate that you create. Creating the emotional climate takes skill and practice. One important concept here is that you are not powerless over your actions and words. If you choose too, you can change.

Some suggestions for improving EQ in the area of self-control

- Asked yourself, "If I express my emotion without thoughtful purpose, what is the risk?" Also asked yourself, "If I express my emotion with doleful purpose, what is the benefit?"
- If you are a person that sits back and watch, practice expressing a positive emotion, such as enthusiasm , in a situation in which you would normally hold back. If you are usually vocal, practice being quiet until you have taken time to get over the immediate reaction.
- Ask a trusted friend to give you input regarding your emotional control. Ask him or her to observe or give you this feedback based on the way you conduct yourself at work, or events.
- The next time you're in a meeting, try on a new behavior related to emotional control. If you normally hold back speaking, express yourself. If you normally do come out with it, discipline yourself by holding back.
- Practice positive emotional expressions. Of you are grateful, let others know.
- Try using the "I feel….." As opposed to "I think…."
- Practice breathing techniques when you feel stressed.
- Mentally stay calm in a crisis.
- Ask yourself, "is this situation truly that bad?"
- Ask yourself, "is my thinking distorted?"
- Think of a time when you felt you lost emotional control. How did it affect you?
- If you ask someone to describe you what were they say?
- Have you ever benefited from expressing positive emotions?
- Think of ways in which you could authentically express positive emotions.
- Has someone ever express positive emotions to you in the workplace. Write down how you felt.
- Think of a time someone express emotions to you in the work place, and it were a negative experience. Write down how you felt.

Exercises for improving self-control

EQ exercise #3: next time

Think about the last time you experience these emotions at work: anxiety, happiness, fear, self-pity, and overwhelmed. List what you actually did at work when you felt these emotions. List how you might have responded better.

EQ exercise #4 music

Self-control creates the emotional climate in which we operate. Imagine emotional climate as a type of music that comes from us. What kind of music or songs do you create? What kind of music or songs you want to create? For example, do you know some people who sound like the blues because every time you are around them, they are whimpering? How about others who seem like they are constantly playing "flight of the bumblebee?" Think about the type of music your emotions make . List the type of music you would like to create.

Self-doubt

Emotional M.O	Typical behavior exhibited
Extrapolator	*The extrapolator is quite skilled at extending one set of events into an entire lifetime vision. The extrapolator will quickly conclude, "if I am unable to do this , then obviously I am unable to do that . if I cannot do A or B, that I've obviously a complete and total failure." A and B may be completely unrelated, but not to the extrapolator. His doubt in one area would naturally cast huge shadows about his ability to perform in another area whatever the truth may be.*
Paralyzed	This person self-doubt simply leaves him or her paralyzed to want to try anything. Avoids moving forward if at all possible, and the fastest way to accomplish that is by simply standing like a deer caught in the headlights.
Defeat through observation	*By observing others fail, he concludes that nothing is possible. He is skilled at finding numerous examples failures that support his claim.*
Prove Myself Wrong	This person works hard to prove him-self wrong and is caught in a never ending cycle of trying to gain proof of accomplishment.

Social Intelligence Practice Lesson

Every culture puts a unique stamp on how people express emotions; the less familiar we are with a given population, the more likely we are to misinterpret their feelings. So we will focus on developing empathy with a diverse range of populations.

Step 1. First Impressions Matter

Write down some things you can do to make a better impression when you encounter someone of the opposite race/culture at work.

_____
_____
_____

Step 2. Courtesy Counts

Write some statements you will say to the public that incorporate daily courtesies.

_____
_____
_____

Step 3. Attitude Is Everything

What are some things you must do to demonstrate an exceptional attitude?

_____
_____
_____

Step 4. Doing the right thing: Ethical issues

Think of a time in which someone requested you to do something unethical. Briefly describe the situation.

_____
_____
_____

Exercise: Listening to yourself at work

Instructions: Over the next several weeks, take time after dealing with the customer to fill out this evaluation form. The customer's interactions may be in person or over the telephone. Take some time at a team meeting to discuss your evaluations with other team members and ask for their feedback.

1. Did I demonstrate interests and friendliness? 1 2 3 4 5 6 7 8 9 10

2. Did I take the initiative in helping resolving the problem? 1 2 3 4 5 6 7 8 9 10

3. Did I call the person by their name at the beginning and end of our exchange? 1 2 3 4 5 6 7 8 9 10

4. Was my overall tone positive? 1 2 3 4 5 6 7 8 9 10

5. Was my tone negative? 1 2 3 4 5 6 7 8 9 10

6. Did my body language give all negative signals? 1 2 3 4 5 6 7 8 9 10

7. Did I listen and let the customer voice their opinion. 1 2 3 4 5 6 7 8 9 10

8. Did I show empathy for the customer? 1 2 3 4 5 6 7 8 9 10

9. Did I use jargon or terms that went over the customer's head? 1 2 3 4 5 6 7 8 9 10

10. Did I thank the customer for his or her business? 1 2 3 4 5 6 7 8 9 10

Worksheet: Empathy is Key

Read through the following statements and circle the most empathetic response.

1. **I can't believe Mr. Smith is making me work third shift. He knows I have children.**

A. Mr. Smith is running a business and we have to do what we have to do.

B. I can understand why you would be upset. Have you tried asking him if he could switch you to an earlier shift?

C. I would be happy if I got third shift since there is a pay differential.

2. **I have too much work on my plate.**

A. I'm sorry you feel overwhelmed by the amount of work you have. Is there any way I can help?

B. That's good since so many people are unemployed right now.

C. Complete the projects you can and discard the rest.

3. **I am so upset. I thought I was going to get the job promotion.**

A. The better candidate got the job.

B. Start spreading rumors about the work performance of the one who got it, and then maybe they will give it to you.

C. I know you are disappointed about not getting the job, but don't give up. There will be a posting of a similar position next week, apply for it.

4. **The regional meeting ran over time, now I will be late for my team meeting.**

A. At least we had time to discuss all of our quarterly goals in the regional meeting.

B. I apologize for you being tardy. Is it possible for John to share with you his notes from the first ten minutes of the meeting?

C. The regional manager is only in town once a quarter, we needed to accommodate her.

5. I am unable to meet my quota this month.

A. Maybe we should promote Sarah to your position.

B. Is that because you were wasting time?

C. Let's talk about why you were unable to meet your quota. What can we do to ensure this does not happen next month?

Social **Intelligence**

Benefits of Emotional Intelligence

• **Decision-making.** Having an awareness of your emotions, where they come from and what they interpret, can help you to take a more rational, well-designed approach to how you are going to make decision.

• **Relationships.** When one is able to understand why they act the way they do and why they react to things the way they do, they tend to gain more of an appreciation for how others act the way they do, which can in turn lead to stronger relationships, law enforcement and personal.

• **Health.** Many times, internal turmoil expresses itself as mental illness. Always harboring negative emotions can lead to higher stress levels in the mind, which can temporarily or fatally damage it.

Giving in Without Giving Up

Compromise is an unavoidable part of associating with others in both the law enforcement and in personal relationships. The ideal situation would be that everyone agrees with everything you say, but that is very unlikely. Unless you live where people don't value diplomacy, this is a skill that will have plenty of opportunities for you to master it.

This can be even more of an issue when you are in a position of less influence. You may be expected to compromise at a greater level or even expected to follow the lead of your superiors, without regard to your own understanding or feelings.

The Balance between Optimism and Pessimism

Extremism may not be a desirable trait in all persons. This is also true when it comes to optimism and pessimism. Being optimistic about every occurrence will potentially lead a person away from reality and taking longer to resolve a situation. It could also give someone a false sense of hope, which will lead to disappointment and could in turn cause the person to abandon all optimism.

Section III
Listening During Service and Effective Communication of Officers

Handout 12-1

Emotion Word Slips (Structured Experience 12-6: Nonverbal Nonsense)

HAPPY	DISPLEASED	IMPATIENT
APPREHENSIVE	DISBELIEVING	SURPRISED
WORRIED	THOUGHTFUL	SKEPTICAL

Training Instrument 11-2

Empathic Listening Observation Checklist

Instructions: This checklist is designed to help you provide feedback to the speaker and the listener during the empathic listening small-group exercise.

Put a check mark in one of the boxes to the right of each statement, depending on whether you observed the behavior as described.

Space is included to share comments with the other participants.

DID THE LISTENER: YES NO NOT SURE

1. Display an open and caring posture? _ _ _

2. Accurately reflect the speaker's feelings? _ _ _

3. Have good eye contact and body language? _ _ _

4. Show interest in the speaker? _ _ _

5. Avoid distracting behaviors? _ _ _

DID THE SPEAKER: YES NO NOT SURE

1. Speak clearly so as to be heard? _ _ _

2. Correct the listener if necessary? _ _ _

3. Have good eye contact and body language? _ _ _

4. Listen when the other was speaking? _ _ _

5. Avoid distracting behaviors? _ _ _

COMMENTS FOR THE SPEAKER AND LISTENER:

AMUSED	ANGRY	FEARFUL
SAD	ANXIOUS	DISAPPOINTED
DISGUSTED	CURIOUS	AWED

LOVING	HORRIFIED	FRANTIC
CONTENTED	EXHAUSTED	BASHFUL
FRUSTRATED	LAZY	FREE
EAGER	PROUD	UNSURE
RELIEVED	CONFUSED	ANNOYED
ALARMED	PAINED/INJURED	ASHAMED

Assessment 11–2

Listening Self-Assessment

Instructions: The purpose of this activity is to help you become a good listener and create an action plan for self-improvement in your listening skills. Place a ✓ in one of the boxes to the right of each item, depending on how you view yourself today. No one will see your ratings unless you share them, so please be honest with yourself.

LISTENING BEHAVIOR	ALWAYS	FREQUENTLY	SOMETIMES	RARELY	NEVER
When another person is speaking to me, I…					
1. Focus on the customer as much as possible.	☐	☐	☐	☐	☐
2. Concentrate on elements of the message.	☐	☐	☐	☐	☐
3. Anticipate the customer's message.	☐	☐	☐	☐	☐
4. Make eye contact with the customer.	☐	☐	☐	☐	☐
5. Not actively listening to the customer.	☐	☐	☐	☐	☐
6. Smile, or give other nonverbal cues.	☐	☐	☐	☐	☐
7. Keep my response to myself.	☐	☐	☐	☐	☐
8. Get distracted by other things in the room.	☐	☐	☐	☐	☐
9. Take notes only on points that are important to me.	☐	☐	☐	☐	☐

10. Nonjudgmental listening or critiquing. ☐ ☐ ☐ ☐ ☐

11. Interrupt the customer in the middle of a phrase. ☐ ☐ ☐ ☐ ☐

12. Think about issues unrelated to the lecture. ☐ ☐ ☐ ☐ ☐

13. Pay attention to the customer body language. ☐ ☐ ☐ ☐ ☐

	ALWAYS	FREQUENTLY	SOMETIMES	RARELY	NEVER
LISTENING BEHAVIOR					
14. Repeat the customer message in my own words.	☐	☐	☐	☐	☐
15. Create my response to fit the situation.	☐	☐	☐	☐	☐
16. Can decipher between fact and opinion.	☐	☐	☐	☐	☐
17. Pretend to be listening when I'm not.	☐	☐	☐	☐	☐
18. Ask questions to clarify the message.	☐	☐	☐	☐	☐
19. Over- reacts to the customer's message.	☐	☐	☐	☐	☐
20. Determine how the customer will react to my response.	☐	☐	☐	☐	☐
21. Clarify meanings of the customer words if I'm unsure about their definitions.	☐	☐	☐	☐	☐
22. Allow customer to vent his or her frustration.	☐	☐	☐	☐	☐
23. Think of different views on the topic.	☐	☐	☐	☐	☐
24. Display an open and caring posture.	☐	☐	☐	☐	☐
25. Create a nonthreatening environment.	☐	☐	☐	☐	☐

Analysis: If you responded "always," "frequently," or "sometimes" for items 3, 7, 8, 11, 12, 17, or 19, these may be areas you need to develop your listening skills, especially your focus on the customer and how you filter information. You may also want to address any of the remaining statements if you responded with "sometimes," "rarely," or "never," particularly items 5, 6, 13, 14, 15, 20, and 23, which directly relate to providing feedback to the customer effectively during a conversation.

Handout 12–2

Argument Analysis (Structured Experience 12–8: Fact or Fiction?)

Argument Analysis

Read through each statement below and answer the three questions that follow with a partner. Be prepared to share your insights with the large group.

The athletic boosters held a cake auction to raise money. We should have a cake auction too.

A. Do we need more information to support the statement?

B. Is the relationship within the statement and the support logical?

C. is there other information about this situation would be helpful to know?

If Dave hadn't laughed so loudly, I wouldn't have spilled my coffee.

A. Do we need more information to support the statement?

B. Is the relationship within the statement and the support logical?

C. is there other information about this situation would be helpful to know?

Jenny seems really organized, and she's good at doing work with a lot of detail to it. She'd be a great project manager.

A. Is there enough information to support the statement?

B. Is the relationship within the statement and the support logical?

C. is there other information about this situation would be helpful to know?

Bill was late to work again today. He's so irresponsible.

A. do we need more information to support the statement?

B. Is the relationship within the statement and the support logical?

C. is there other information about this situation would be helpful to know?

All four of those candidates for the job are graduates of State University. They have Such high-quality programs that I'm sure any of them would do well.

A. do we need more information to support the statement?

B. Is the relationship within the statement and the support logical?

C. is there other information about this situation would be helpful to know?

Our profits were up last year by 7 percent and up by 5 percent the year before that. We should certainly have higher profits again this year.

A. do we need more information to support the statement?

B. Is the relationship within the statement and the support logical?

C. is there other information about this situation would be helpful to know

Section IV

Elements of Effective Law Enforcement Leadership Practices

The Police Department: ethics and code of conduct minimize ethical ambiguities by communicating guidelines for employees to apply when making decisions. They serve as the organizations conscious. This section explains the difference between a code of ethics, any code of conduct, summarizes their prevalence and content, and describes how to use a code of ethics to assess and improve ethical performance.

Have you ever had a really difficult day? The kind of day at any given time a situation can go from mediocre too difficult to worse? You may not realize it, but your attitude might be the problem. We don't have to say anything to anybody to communicate with them. And, our body language will transmit negative emotions to others. The raising of our eyebrows, we often find those negative emotions reflected back at us.

Because the public has such a low starting opinion of law enforcement in general, particularly when problems occur in the neighborhood, it doesn't take much to push an interaction into a downward spiral of negativism. If your job is to handle complaints on a regular basis, you must learn how to communicate effectively. If you don't learn to control how you interact with the public, it will cause more than just your performance to suffer. Your overall attitude on a personal level will likely erode, damaging relationships in the sector you patrol. You will eventually become desperately unhappy in your job. Unfortunately, this leads to officers or civil service workers judging many people unfairly. It is extremely easy for a person who is being perfectly honest to be perceived as dishonest or as hiding something.

How to determine moral climate

(a) Identifying moral problems,

(b) Choosing criteria for resolving moral conflicts, and

(c) Evaluating the moral correctness of outcomes that ensue from departmental decisions.

Since atmosphere is a function of how employees collectively perceive and interpret elements of the work atmosphere, atmosphere can be thought of as an intervening variable. As such it provides the necessary link between departmental processes and police officer behavior.

There are 5 factors that interact to determine the moral climate in the Police Department:

Goal emphasis

(Developing norms for selecting department goals), means emphasis

(Developing norms for determining how departmental goals should be attained),

Reward orientation

(Developing norms regarding how performance is rewarded),

Task support

(Developing norms regarding how resources are created to perform specific tasks). And Socio-emotional support.

Developing norms regarding the type of relationships expected in the department .

It becomes obvious that police supervisors and department heads are responsible for developing a positive moral climate within the police department. The literature on leadership strategy, departmental transformation, police ethics and public social contract provides support for a claim that moral climate in the department emerges mainly from the way in which key departmental processes transmit departmental heads expectations about the moral climate – the way officers and civil service workers should handle responsibility, equity, or serving the interests of the public. Therefore, police departmental heads expectations about moral behavior of their officers or civil service workers will significantly influence moral climate of a particular police department or law enforcement institution.

Two main dimensions of trust:

(a) Cognition-based trust, which relies on appraisals of peers or subordinates professional competence and reliability;

(b) Affect or emotion-based trust, which is present when an officer feel save to share his/her personal feelings and personal frustrations, believing that the other party would respond constructively and supportively.

In the 127police enclave, we could mention this notion of trust to include trust between the police and the community. It is important to note that all of the above-described factors intermingle with each other in predicting ethical or unethical behaviors.

Let us use trust as an example. In an police department with strong moral climate, composed of individuals with good character, it is safe to assume that high level of trust will promote ethical behavior. In such Police Department's, officers who trust others (both cognitively and emotionally) and feel trusted by other police officers will be reluctant to violate this trust by engaging in unethical behavior. On the other hand, if the moral climate is low, and poor leadership examples exist, with a lot of structural holes and many cliques; it is very likely that high level of trust within a deviant clique will promote unethical behavior

Therefore, to set a climate conductive to ethical behavior in police department, police department heads have to consider all of the above factors. To summarize, they have to foster character development and moral habits of police officers by educating and training them in police ethics; establish high moral climate through appropriate use of goals, rewards, and facilitate development of strong and networks within the department, extending into the community; and establish both cognitive-based and affect-based trust among all departmental staff and between the police and the public they serve. In doing so, the department heads will not only facilitate ethical behavior of their officers; they will also prevent or at least lessen the strength of the infamous police subculture, so typical of paramilitary policing. In trying to achieve the above goals, police department heads will immediately discover that, first, setting their own example is of the utmost importance, and second, that ethics does not only apply to police officers' dealings with the public, but also to their own dealings with their subordinates.. The quality of policing in a democratic society relies on the quality of the people doing the work. Policing should strive to achieve a virtue of integrity of all police officers and supervisors, including department heads.

INTEGRITY

Researchers have discovered that integrity is a central trait of effective law enforcement leaders, while interpersonal and group relationship researchers have identified integrity as a central determinant of trust in police departments. Integrity is also central to the mission of policing. Integrity is not only the highest achievement there can be in a human life, but also the most difficult. So what exactly is integrity?

"Character, the established habit of doing right where there is no one to make you do it but yourself". Integrity is "irreplaceable as the foundation. A person of integrity is somebody who has reasonably coherent and relatively stable set of core moral values and virtues.

Integrity is loyalty, in action, to rational principles and values. Integrity is the principle of, practicing what one preaches. Not allowing any irrational consideration to overwhelm one's rational convictions". Integrity in policing, means that a police officer or civil service worker genuinely accepts value and moral standards of policing, and that he consistently acts, out of his own will, in accordance with those values, standards, and virtues, even in the face of internal or external pressures .

Let's describes five personality types that lack integrity.

The first is the moral chameleon, a person who is overly anxious to please others, while not being resistant to social pressure, thus willing to quickly abandon, bend or modify previously avowed principles.

The second is the moral opportunist, whose values are also loosely selective, based on their own short-term self-interest.

The third type is the Moral hypocrite, an individual who has two sets of values. One set of virtues for public consumption and another set for actual use as a moral code.

The fourth is the morally weak- who has a coherent set of core virtues, but usually lacking the courage to act on those core virtues.

The final type is the moral self-deceiver, a person who thinks of themselves as acting on a set of moral principles, while, in fact, he does not. It is everyone's moral obligation to change one's views if one finds that some idea he holds is wrong. It is a breach of integrity to know that one is right and then proceed to defy the right in practice.

Why do some people have little integrity?

Why is it so hard to achieve it?

First, everyone is not rational. Integrity requires the discipline of purpose, carefully choosing the means to one's ends, and making full use of that knowledge.

Second,(when you squeeze an orange you can only get out of it orange what's inside). (Therefore when you pressure a person you can only get out of them what's inside). A person may lack integrity because his desires are inconsistent with his moral values. If a person, when under temptation, act upon the moment, he will indeed lack integrity. The same is true when an irrational fear drives it officer's behavior. An individual's integrity will be question if he does not put rational principles into practice simply out of inertia.

Third, probably the most common reason an officer may lack integrity is that he succumbs to peer pressure. Peer pressure may come from several sources (e.g., department head, co-workers, public, or spouse) and take several forms (e.g., physical intimidation or verbal and nonverbal disapproval). A officer with high integrity will not allow popularity to take priority over rational decisions.

CONCLUSION

From the above discussion, it should be obvious that integrity can only be achieved if an officer strives to achieve it. Appropriate education and training in police ethics, good moral climate in the police department , appropriate social networks (both within the department and within the public we serve), trust and support, can all motivate police officers to strive for integrity and help them achieve it. I believe that, once achieved, integrity of police officers is one of the most important steps toward professionalization of policing, and one of the most powerful antidotes to police corruption, brutality, neglect of human rights, and other forms of police deviance.

Police ethics provides a moral compass to both police officers and department heads, by specifying the core imperatives, values, and virtues of policing, by delineating the process of moral reasoning and decision-making, by setting the standards of police ethical conduct, and by defining the means and the content of police ethics education and training. Law enforcement department heads have to collaborate in developing police ethics. Developing and implementing police ethics invokes changes in police the department . Police department heads and practitioners are entrusted with developing police ethics, therefore, themselves should be persons of high integrity.

Element 1: Assess your current culture

The first step to building a committed culture is to assess your department's status and then direct the energy towards commitment. High performing department heads measure two dimensions of culture: **purpose and people architect.**

Measuring purpose

Purpose is the sum and integration of the departments may heal betting to in mission, vision, and values. It is the extent to which officers and civil service workers understand and share their department vision.

Measuring people architecture

People architecture is the alignment between the department's purpose and its reward and evaluation system.

    To measure your department's people architecture, first taking inventory of the reward and evaluation system used to motivate employees. Then consider the extent to which the systems support your department's vision, mission, and values. If these two issues are not aligned, and if the incentive system contradicts your department purpose then the culture would not support itself. It becomes like a car with both the break and the gas pedals pressed at the same time. At best, the call goes nowhere. At worst, serious damage occurs. A coincidental culture spells real trouble in turbulent times. It can fall apart at the first bump in the role and whether the bump is an undulation or speedbump it doesn't really matter.

    For example this type of culture often arises when new leaders try to select people with the right values. In contrast to all the other culture types, the committed culture merges both purpose and people architecture to create a culture where police officers and civil service workers understand and believe in the vision of the department , and are encouraged and rewarded for making it happen.

Element 2: Create a shared purpose

Many factors go into creating a shared purpose, including officers and civil service workers understanding of the department's values and vision, and agreement with those values and vision.

Defining values

The **first** of these issues concerning understanding requires a department to have clearly defined values. Many police departments find themselves rudderless when it comes to their sense of who they are and what they stand for. Most officers and civil service workers, especially the really talented ones need to know who you are and what you're about. "Talented officers and civil service workers are looking for a values fit" with their department heads. Without it, they will not work for you. They'll leave. **Second**, values define what is and what is not acceptable it creates the department's code of behavior. Making decisions without a code of behavior, particularly the kind of decision that are often require in <u>**volatile times**</u>, can be much more difficult or even dangerous.

Therefore, the first exercise is for leadership to engage officers and civil service workers in creating a list of values that define what the department stands for. These values should be very powerful, and provide a strong bond leaking every officer and civil service worker in the department defining values is more than putting words on paper. Most departments have mission statements. But many do not follow them. While you may never hear Reeboks mission statement when you buy a pair of sneakers, you know what Reebok is all about.

Here are some techniques that you may use

Use orientation and training programs that emphasize department values

Both structured and unstructured opportunities to socialize with officers and civil service workers

"Storytelling" events and department histories that dramatize guiding values

Element 3: Align the people architect

Developing a share purpose is only part of building a committed culture. The other part is the alignment of the people architect, including the award systems and evaluation systems. The only way officers and civil service workers will fulfill the vision is to share the vision. The award system is the mechanisms that make the difference reality.

The **first** element is designing a complete and working award system to carefully align with the values, mission, and vision of the organization. Systems that reward behavior that's not related to the mission can play havoc with a department.

The **second** element of a completely aligned award system is to reward behavior that is under the officer's control. Tying incentives to uncontrollable events, rather than manageable behavior, only leaves officers and civil service workers frustrated. Not every law enforcement officer or civil service worker is equally motivated by money. Nor profit is always the driving force in a department. The key is to identify your department driving force and key values, then create a matrix to measure performance on those issues.

Evaluation systems

Evaluation systems should be closely tied to reward systems and drive the type, level, and distribution of awards.

The questions supervisors must ask when designing evaluation systems are:

Who do we want to evaluate?

What competencies and criteria do we want to evaluate?

Do we want to evaluate officers or civil service workers on their ability to satisfied customers?

A committed culture cannot be created when officers or civil service workers are told the department values one set of behaviors but measures another. In departmental leadership, what and how you measure becomes a de facto statement of what you value and stand for. This means both internal customers those who come into the office to pay traffic fines or court fees and the external customer the one that deals directly with the law enforcement officers on our city streets. **Keep it simple.** This advice does not imply that a culture of commitment is easy to build, or that its infrastructure will necessarily be simple. I am providing your department with a compass that will guide you through turbulent times; high-performing department heads rely on simple and clear value statements and unambiguous incentives.

Average leaders tend to be invisible; the best leaders frequently walk around and strike up conversations with their staff, asking about their families and other personal matters. They also let it be known that they want to be informed, creating an atmosphere of openness that makes it easier for communication to take place.

Place a T or F for true or false next to each number

1. Does leadership demand certain toughness?

2. A common failing of leaders, from shift supervisors to department heads, is the failure to be empathetically assertive when necessary?

3. One sign of an assertive department head or shift supervisor is the ability to say no firmly and definitively.

4. When someone consistently performs poorly, despite all attempts at helpful feedback and development, officer has to be confronted directly and openly?

5. This describes the petty tyrant our office bully? The glorification of leaders who are selfish, arrogant, and brash, ignores the calls of the department ?

6. During hard times, shift supervisors need to call on whatever reserve of goodwill they may have built up over time?

7. Having the ability to keep wrong, unrestrained desire for power under control is one mark of a mature supervisor?

8. When people fail to perform, the supervisor's task is to give helpful feedback rather than let the experience and the lapse go unnoticed?

9. Persuasion, consensus building, and all the other elements of influence do not always do the job?

10. Realizing that unity and cohesiveness are built from personal bonds, the best supervisors organized downtime events like softball games and awards celebrations and make a point of playing or celebrating themselves?

The leader is responsible for ethics or norms that govern the behavior of people in the departments. Department heads set the tone.

Ethics and leadership go hand-in-hand. An ethical environment is conducive to effective supervision, and effective supervision is conducive to ethics. Effective supervision is a consequence of ethical conduct and ethical conduct is a consequence of effective supervision.

Thus, it is most important that department heads be aware of their considerable influence on the ethical climate of their people and act accordingly. The department head needs to do three things:

1. Achieve an understanding of ethics

2. Serve as a role model in making ethical decisions

3. Develop and implement a plan of action for promoting ethical conduct on the part of their staff.

I firmly believe that any police department, in order to survive need to believe in and enforce the lead by example principal, a sound set based on policies and actions. Next, the most important factor in law enforcement success is faithful adherence to those beliefs. And finally, if a law enforcement or civil service department meet the challenge of reaching their goals, they must be prepared to change everything about itself except those beliefs as it develops a legal moral compass.

What I'm referring specifically to this set of beliefs:

Respect for the individual-to respect the dignity and rights of each person in the department.

Public service-to give the best public service of any law enforcement agency in the world

Every law enforcement organization is guided by certain beliefs or values. These values communicate to all members whether sworn officers or civil service workers "what we stand for" and "what is important to us". Whether the values are explicit are only implicit, they constitute the essence of the Departments credo and leadership philosophy.

In short, we have never been, and still are not, a collection of private individuals who, except for a conscious contract to create a minimal government, having nothing in common. Our lives makes sense in 1000 ways, most of which we are unaware of, because of traditions that are centuries if not millennia, old. It is these traditions that help us to know that it does make a difference who we are and how we treat one another.

American values make us who we are. They contribute to our basic beliefs about the nature of the good life, provide us direction giving meaning to our lives. Values shape what is called a national character. Our laws are rooted in traditional American values and, over time, as the values change, the laws are modified.

Read this material on American values. Ponder it over and reflect on the importance of his meaning. Then decide for yourself: is this an adequate representation of American values? If not, what changes would you propose?

>
> **Democracy**
> **Justice**
> **Human rights**
> **Equality**
> **Freedom**
> **Responsibility**
> **Reason**
> **Diversity of opinion**
> **Quality of life**
> **World peace**

What Should Be Done

Development of a plan of action for promoting ethical conduct

A.   purpose

1. What is the mission of the larger department of which you are a part of?

2. What is the mission of your department/ unit?

B Values

1. What are the principal values of the larger department of which you are a part?

2. What are the principal values that you want to promote in your department/ unit?

B.   **Code of Ethics**

Formulate a code of ethics for your department/ unit in the form of guiding principles.

1.

2.

3.

4.

5.

6.

7.

8.

9.

10.

D.   **Developing an Ethics Program**

Outline what you would include in an ethics program for promoting ethical conduct in your department. Consider the following possibilities: orientation program for new officers or civil service workers, ethics seminar for department heads, participative decision-making, open door policy, including ethics issues as an agenda item instead of meetings, and an annual ethics review.

In America's current relativistic culture where everyone wants to use different standards and where every situation is supposed to require its own code of conduct, is promising to hope that people from every culture designed to live and quickly can agree on one standard. Take a look at the result of some of the research that shows how many variations on the golden rule exist:

Christianity: whatever you want men to do to you, do also to them.

Islamic: no one of you is a believer until he loves for his neighbor what he loves for himself.

Judaism: what is hateful to you, do not do to your fellow man. This is the entire law; all the rest is commentary.

Buddhism: hurt not others with that which weighs pains yourself.

Hinduism: this is the sum of duty; do not unto others what you would not have them do unto you.

Zoroastrianism: whatever is disagreeable to yourself, do not do onto others.

Confucianism: what you do not want done to yourself, do not do to others.

Bahai: and if thine eyes be turned towards justice, choose thou for thy neighbor that which thou choose for thyself.

Jainism: a man shall wonder about treating all creatures as he himself would be treated.

Yoruba Proverb (Nigeria): one going to take a pointed stick to pinch a baby bird should

Try it on him-self to feel how it hurts.

There are two important points when referring to ethics. The first is a standard to follow. The second is the will to follow it.

The Golden Rule

How do you rate yourself when it comes to ethics? A man who is not honest with himself presents a hopeless case. Categorize using the following five statements.

1. I'm always ethical.

2. I am mostly ethical.

3. I am somewhat ethical.

4. I'm seldom ethical.

5. I'm never ethical.

Can you imagine someone saying, "Please treat me worse than I treat you"? Not, everyone wants to be treated well. It is not unreasonable for any person to desire good treatment from others. Nor is it asking too much to expect people to treat others well. It is very difficult for people to justify demanding better treatment from others than they give. What can they base it on? Riches? If that's the case, then the person making $100,000 a year who desires good treatment from someone making $25,000 must agree to be treated poorly by those who make $500,000!

You can see where this can go. No matter what arbitrary criteria you can think of whether it's wealth, talent, ideology, nationality, race, or something else it cannot be greatly supported. While the first rules in human relations is to seek common ground with others. That is a good guideline whether you are exploring a new friendship, making an arrest, connecting with children, arguing with your spouse.

Professional Blinders

To the man with a hammer, every problem is a nail. We each carry on favorite tool. Some people choose a line of work because they think is important; others think their work is important because they've chosen it. In either case, there is a possible temptation to translate every problem into one's own bailiwick. The lawyer sees every problem as a legal problem; the artist concentrates on the aesthetic dimensions; the nutritionist thinks it all can be explained by looking at our diets. Academics are among the worst culprits. They plow one narrow strip of their field all their lives and insist that everything of important grows right there in their own pasture. The businessman: no matter what they say, the bottom line is the bottom line. It's all business. I don't care if it's international politics. It's all about money. I'm not saying it's right or wrong. I'm saying that's how it is.

Character Counts

Your personality will never be greater than your character. Character is a key to living a life of integrity and ethical excellence.

- **Character is more than talk:** many people talk about doing the right thing, the action is a true measure of character pit. Dennis colostomy, the CEO of Tyco, often shrouded the fugal way he conducted business and talk about the Spartan offices the company maintained. However, anyone who watched his actions closely could have seen that his talk and Walk lineup.

- **Talent is a gift-: character is a choice:** there are a lot of things in life a person doesn't get to choose, where you're born, who your parents or, how tall you are. But there are some important things every person does choose. We choose our religion, our attitude, and our character.

- **Character brings lasting success with people:** trust is essential when working with the public. Character engenders trust.

- **People cannot rise above the limitations of their character:** there are really only three kinds of people. Those who don't succeed those who achieve success temporarily, and those who become and remain successful. Having character is the best way to sustain success. No matter how talented are rich people are, they would not be able to out run their character.

- **The more people get involved, the greater the pressure for conformity:** ethical decisions made in private have their own pressure, one may be tempted to believe that a private indiscretion will not become public information. Public decisions involving other people carry a different kind of pressure than that of conformity. No matter what level of pressure there is, you can't allow you peers to force you into making of unethical decisions.

- **Inaction is also a decision:** some people's reaction to ethical decision-making is to avoid taking any action. It's important to recognize that inaction is also a decision. But for every Cynthia Cooper, who step forward and told world.com board about the company's shady accounting practices, there are thousands of people who choose every day not to act when they see officers or civil service workers cut corners or compromise ethics-and who ultimately will live with the consequences.

Define your group membership as either the dominant group other sub dominant group, and then examine how membership in this group impacts workplace performance.

Dominate/Subordinate
Group Dynamics

Category	Dominate/ Majority Group	Subordinate/ Minority Group
Resources	Has access to resources	needs access to resources
Rules	Makes the rules	adjust to the rules
Resources	Control resources	Needs access to resources
Culture	Define the culture	Struggle to fit in
Truth	Defines the truth	has their truth and Experience question Invalidated
Normal	viewed as normal	viewed as inferior are as Exception to the group
Capable	Assumed to be Capable (qualified)	Often assumed to be deficient (not qualified)
Benefit of doubt	given the benefit Of doubt	has to earn the benefit of doubt (has to prove they Or qualified)
Awareness of group Membership	Unaware of group dynamics	Very aware of group dynamics
Since a word	seeing their group As the smartest	Internalized dominate group beliefs reflected in Lack of self-worth, low self Esteem or self-confidence
Behavior	Encourages subordinate Group members To assimilate	Adopts; develops behavior pleasing are accepting to dominate group members And cannot "show-up" too Authentic are genuine

Treatment	least aware of Differential Treatment	mostly aware of differential treatment
Discrimination	Sees incidents of Discrimination as Individual actions That has little to Do will group Membership	Sees patterns of group level behavior based on repetitive nature

White privilege exercise

Members of the dominant group are often not aware of the special status they have over subordinate grows.(Called the invisible backpack of privilege)s. White privileged experimental exercise emphasizes many subtle aspects of white privilege in American society.

All participant line up with their backs to a wall, and up to 50 statements is subsequently read aloud. Read the statement, participants who answer affirmatively take one step forward. Typically, after the last day many European-American males are several steps ahead of the other social groups. Participants then turn around face each other and expressed their feelings about the exercise.

Sample statements include:

1. I can turn on the television, open to the front page of the newspaper and see people of my race or gender widely represented in a positive manner.

2. I can do well in a challenging situation without being called a credit to my race or gender.

3. I can be pretty sure that if I ask to talk to the person in charge I will be facing a person of my race and gender.

To live an ethical life, you must hold to your principles as you make tough decisions. Ethical principle is a compass forever fixed, that is as important in law enforcement as it is in civil customer service. I believe there is a wealth that is greater than money, and it comes from how you interact with others. People who practice the golden rule treat others with dignity and respect and can be content in the knowledge that they are living an ethical life. Giving truly is the highest level of living. It makes the world a better place. And it also makes for better law enforcement and customer service.

Finding your ethical code

Read item 1-11 below. On another sheet of paper, write the number after each item that describes you best. Using this rating scale:

1= rarely   2= sometimes   3= most of the time

1. I can hold a belief even of others pressure me to give it up.	1	2	3
2. I'm responsible and keep my promise.	1	2	3
3. I am impartial.	1	2	3
4. I am very patient.	1	2	3
5. I am generous and kind.	1	2	3
6. I use logical decision-making.	1	2	3
7. My life has order and transparent.	1	2	3
8. I am loyal and devoted to people and ideas.	1	2	3
9. I am courageous and bound by my beliefs.	1	2	3
10. I am humble and conservative.	1	2	3
11. I use care before making decisions.	1	2	3

Add other characteristics that are important to you. Together, all these characteristics form the foundation of your code of ethics. Add up your points. The higher your point total, the more these characteristics are part of your ethical code.

Assessment 11 - 1

Leadership self-assessment

Instructions: For each bullet sub-competency, rate your own strength by marking **H** (high) **M** (medium) **L** (low). After you have rated each of the bullet items, returned to the competency and give you an overall rating (high, medium, and low).

Interwork: self-awareness   rating_____

- Develop clarity of personal values, and vision   rating_____
- Develop and execute a personal strategy   rating_____
- Demonstrate authenticity through   rating_____
  Values and vision.
- Take accountability for my leadership actions   rating_____
- Knowledge when someone has done well   rating_____
- Learn new technology devices   rating_____

Inner work, resiliency   rating_____

- Be willing to jump in and get things done   rating_____
- Build on others ideas for the benefit of the department   rating_____
- Maintain appropriate attitude   rating_____
- Persistence in overcoming adversity   rating_____
- Act proactively in seeking new opportunities   rating_____
- Persistently rise task   rating_____

Working with others (department heads, subordinates, peers):   rating_____
Interpersonal and relationship skills

- Understand and appreciate diversity   rating_____
- Participate and contribute fully as a leader   rating_____

- Demonstrate empathy and understanding   rating_____
- Build trust and demonstrate trustworthiness   rating_____

Working with others (supervisors, subordinates, peers)
civil service workers)   rating_____
- Motivate staff to high performance   rating_____
- review for development and improve performance   rating_____
- Lead with appreciation and respect for diversity of individual   rating_____
  Values and needs
- Delegate task equally and with awareness of appropriateness   rating_____

Responsibilities

Working with others (external} public orientation   rating_____
- Understand public needs and expectations   rating_____
- Gather customer requirements and input   rating_____
- communicate effectively with the public   rating_____
- Monitor performance standards   rating_____

The challenge of change: create, support, and manage change   rating_____

- Understand improvement initiatives (three levels: managing your all transition/transformation, supervising a department

- Identify and implement change initiatives/efforts   rating_____
- Promote and support for change initiatives   rating_____
- Understand return on investment relating to ethics   .   rating_____
- Guiding and supporting staff
- Support staff in navigating through   rating_____
  departmental change
- Support staff in navigating challenges   rating_____
  Demonstrate and build resilience in the face of adversity   rating_____

Training instrument 11 -2

Instructions: In the spaces below, identify your leadership strengths and weaknesses.

- I believe that my most capable leadership strengths are:

- Others believe that my most capable leadership strengths are:

- I believe that I need to develop the following leadership competencies:

- Others believe that I need to develop the following leadership competencies:

- I choose to develop a strategy for working with others for this competency (instead of growing it myself):

Handout 11-2

Mike's Role

You are Mike and this is your story:

"I always tried to finish my work on time, the last week I had the flu and worried it could be that anthrax thing because I open a junk mail envelope from Florida. With all this terrorist business, I cannot focus on my work and had to get some counseling. And all Angela did was yelled at me for not finishing the tables for the monthly report. That woman is obsessed with trivial details. Nobody reads those reports anyhow and who cares if it is late by a couple of days?"

Angela Role:

You are Angela and this is your story:

"Mike never finishes anything before the deadline. We both agree when his part of the task is to be completed, but he is always late and always with a handy excuse. Last month his kid was sick. This month he had the flu. He has my sympathy but I expect my coworkers to behave in a professional manner. He also complains that nobody read the monthly reports anyhow, but it is not our job to make policy, is it?"

Handout 11 - 4

Observation Checklist

Instructions: From your perspective, what was the crux of this conflict? Record observations in the spaces below.

1. Did Mike and Angela seem more eager to talk or listen?

2. What types of active listening behaviors did you notice?

3. What are some examples of negative behaviors and emotions (such as accusations),

4. (Betrayal, domination, hostility, anger, frustration, and sarcasm) that you observed in the conversation between Mike and Angela?

5. What are some examples of positive behavior and emotions (such as understanding, apology, empathy, support, and hope) that you observed in the conversation between Mike and Angela?

6. How did Mike and Angela demonstrate their ability to use self- mediation techniques related to the following checklist items?

Pre-Assignment

Complete this worksheet before the class begins. Makes note of what you hope to learn or goals you want to address after the class.

1) In your own words, what is social intelligence? Have you ever heard this term before?
   _____
   _____
   _____

2) Why is social intelligence important at home and work?
   _____
   _____
   _____

3) What areas of social intelligence would you be more interested in learning about?
   _____
   _____
   _____

4) What do you hope to learn or take away from this class?
   _____
   _____
   _____

Any other thoughts:
_____
_____
_____
_____
_____
_____

➢ Gather information and analyze the conflict

➢ Establish mutual goals

➢ Brainstorm strategies for achieving the goals

➢ Debrief

Module Two: Increase Your Social Intelligence

Social self-control is demonstrated by an officer being able to manage his or her distressing feelings. Officers who are competent in social intelligence stay composed, calm, and unflappable in stressful situations, regardless of the environment. They have control of their emotions rather than the perpetrator having control of them. Their emotions and behaviors functioning stay intact. We wonder why the situations around us don't, he reason is because we are relying on the people around us to change. But being aware of our own actions and behaviors is one of the keys to changing ourselves, and our surroundings. We must alert ourselves of verbal communication or body language we are putting out and how our behaviors can cause others to react aggressively.

Remove or Limit Self-Deception

Self-deception is a tool we commonly use to try and hide something from ourselves or prevent ourselves from accepting something. We can often try to make ourselves believe what ever we want and alter facts it on mine by self deceiving ourselves. No one is exempt from this habit and we can find ourselves practicing it more often than we think. Four instance, we can self deceive ourselves to believe the people are so different such as, Music, Sports, and other forms of entertainment. That they couldn't possibly have anything in common with you. Self deception can affect our relationships with others and give people the wrong impression of ourselves. One of the simplest ways we can help prevent this type of deception it Is to simply be honest with ourselves and others.

Always communicate clearly what you mean without ambiguity. (say what you mean but don't say it mainly). When taking information, review the facts before making a conclusion. Recognize facts and notices the difference in the environment. Are people receiving you as being angry, is a crowd beginning to form. Is the person being arrested resisting and if the person is not resisting are you aware of how much force you are using and is excessive the force necessary. Not just because you are afraid but because the force is needed. Officers must take charge of the area once they arrive on the scene. While it is alright to have confidence and esteem by believing in the law or relieving you know what is best, it is not beneficial to usurp your authority or to deceive yourself into thinking over the blue line of ethical behavior, since it can't cause you to damage your future relationship with the public.One of the simplest ways we can help prevent this type of deception is to simply be honest with ourselves and the people in the district in which we work.

There are three key reasons for deception:

These self deceptive ideas are made automatically without the benefit of critical thinking.

Once made, the expectations are no longer examined for the accuracy realism.

These unrealistic self-deceptions or adhered to as the Golden rule clung and to tediously

Conditioning/socialization Developing CI's

We often forget one of the easiest tools to increase our own social intelligence is to increase your presence and within the sector/district you patrol. It doesn't have to be a lengthy or complicated process and can be done very professionally or casually. The people around your sector/ district can see your usual actions and behaviors and can give an honest opinion about them. The thought of asking someone to inform you about all another members of their community can seem unnerving and even downright scary, but the information provided by the community can prove to be invaluable. When the situation allows get out of your police car and talk person-to-person with the people in your district. Don't be afraid of the community in which you work, remember every good officer has a 'CI' in their community. Someone who can tell them what's going on in the neighborhood. If possible, let the person know in advance when you will want information or ideas of how better you can serve their community. Give them time to mentally process the information so later they have time to form an opinion and gather the type of information. A random request for feedback (such as right after an incident) can be acceptable too, but keep in mind the person may be caught off guard and or are stressed out and may not be able to provide useful information right away. When civilians express their concerns too early, they generate fewer facts and often give poor or inaccurate information. But when the public takes the time and response in a thoughtful way the outcome is better.

The most important part about asking your CI for information is your relationship with that person and to prepare yourself for what you may hear. Remember the police officer has the most scrutinize job in the free world, and there will be incomplete and inaccurate information at times. Take the advice and tips that the person offers as tools to help you improve your service to the community. Don't turn defensive or angry just because the person delivering the information may have said something you don't agree with.

Be Open to Change

Humans are designed to be creatures of habit, nobody wants to be handcuffed or have their freedom taken away. Officers have the authority to threaten someones freedom or take their life. We must understand the police force did not always have the urban communites best interest in mind once they arrived on location. The police department was used to keep people of color in their place during the civil rights movent.

 Young officers often have the mindset that because they wear a badge people will automatically conform to what we say. (only a rookie believe this nonsense) everyone wants to make a clean arrest, but if something throws a kink in our routine, we tin to lose control and in the heat of the moment we pull our fire arm when it isn't necessary or physically batter the person out of frustration.

But being open to change allows officers to adapt to their new surroundings and situations and helps them grow as a police officer and a person. Changing our attitude about ourselves and others can help determine how we build our connections within the communtiy we serve. Sometimes after we receive feedback from the public, we may need to change our communication style and become less aggressive in non-aggressive situations. Perhaps after speaking with the people living in your sector/ district you decide you need to change how you communicate and reciprocate what is being communicated to you. Whatever the reason, it is important to not disregard the importance of your willingness to change and not turn a blind eye to its prospects. Changing how we see ourselves and the people that surround us can have a positive impact on our attitudes and can help build better relationships with the community we serve. Police officers must understand the inner city and urban community view law-enforcement from a holistic perspective. Meaning they view law enforcement from the time they're put in handcuffs all the way through the court process. They understand that when the police arrive on location they would not be treated fairly and if arrested they would have to go through a grueling court process in a biases court system.

Tips for accepting change:

- Determine how the change can benefit you
- Don't assume a need for change is negative
- Recognize that change is a chance for improvement

Learn not to need to react

While developing a CI in the sector/ district you serve can be a great tool to use, but knowing the district for ourselves can be just as valuable. Learn to refect on your past experiences. Being reflective will give you a chance to learn from your past experiences (as well as your mistakes) and recognize it is a teachable moment and a chance for learning valuable communication techniques. By reflecting on our actions, we can see first hand what actions we took, how they played out, and what kind of effect they had on the situation. Use your six senses to recreate an experience in your mind and the actions that you took.

What behaviors did you demonstrate?

What was going through your mind at the time?

How do the people around you respond?

Think about the body language you used and make note of any cues you may have seen in others because of the body language you used. What intuitions or gut feelings do you feel from the experience? Do you feel as though you have learned anything new are useful from the experience? These steps and process can help you reflect back on your actions and increase not only your self-awareness, but your awareness of others.

Case Study

Officer Jones wants to become more self-aware of his actions and how he comes across to people. He is speaking for the first time at a small conference held at his office building. He's pretty nervous, but he asks a coworker, Bobby, to watch him speech and give him some feedback on it when he's through. When it was over, officer Jones met up with Bobby and asked him what he thought. Bobby was able to offer him several compliments on his delivery and attitude, but he also had some helpful hints about the items in the speech and how he used them. At first, Officer Jones was hurt, but when he reflected back on his actions and what Bobby said, he realized he was right and just trying to help. So Officer Jones decided to research some new topic ideas and better prepare himself for the next speech he would have to give sometime in the future.

Module Three: The Keys to Empathy

Empathy is one of our most significant interpersonal skills because it allows officers to reciprocate what's the other person is saying and communicate more effectively with the community they serve. We know empathy can simply mean to 'put ourselves in the other person's shoes', but it can also mean to take an active role in getting to know the people in your sector/ District and treating them with the respect they deserve.

Outside circumstances and people do not have to dictate how officers will behave. It is said that an police officer can feel the suffering of the community he serves, **term as emotional resonance** that could produce burnout. Officers don't need to feel the suffering of their District in order to be motivated to act compassionately and to try to help relieve their pain. Which is referred to as **discriminating or discerning awareness**. While officers are capable of appreciating others pain, it should be accompanied by **discernment**. If officers are totally overwhelmed by others pain, then they can be paralyzed by it. A degree of distance **balance** is required to be able to perform your role as a police officer. Officers need to cultivate strong courage to work for the benefit of others.

Example:

Suppose your not a police officer and you have a wife and a child. You have been looking for work for two months and finally you have an inteview. Your walking down the street wearing your only dress shirt and pair of new slacks. A police car aggressively pulls in front of you. The officer draws his gun and demands that you put your hands in the air and lay on the ground. Your resume papers are blowing away, your freshly pressed white dress shirt is now covered with dirt and your now late for you job interview. As a tax paying citizen how do you feel about the incident.

Internal versus external control

Listening is considered a skill that all police officers must learn to cultivate, so like any other skill it must be implemented and strengthened through practice. Listening allows officers to understand the complaint and understand what the person is talking about and register what they are trying to communicate. Building better listening skills starts with learning to pay attention when someone speaks and actively listening to what they are saying. Key tips to help accomplish this are to give your attention to the person by facing them and making eye contact. **Don't usurp your authority**. You'll find that you will catch more of what the person is saying and be able to retain more. Paying attention and building better listening skills can show that you care about what they have to say and this method can help build rapport with them. Internal and external control are different, but related matters that are essential for a balance in police work. **(The Warrior VS The Guardian)**

Tips for better listening skills:

- Remove any distractions
- Make eye contact with the person speaking
- Nod your head periodically
- Ask for follow up details or information
- Ask the person to repeat anything you may have missed

Don't profile

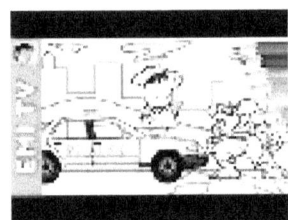

No matter how many times we hear the old phrase "Don't profile people" or "It's not our place to profile", we more than likely find ourselves doing it anyway – we just don't want to admit it. Whether subconsciously or not, we still find ourselves profiling certian culture groups or races. Whether it is based on their clothes, job title, the way they talk or walk, gender, hair color, skin color, and etc. When someone is talking loud or sagging their pants, what do you think in your head? Do you automatically make comments on how they present themselves or the way they dress is subpar to the group. Of course you would never say this out loud or tell them directly, but you have already maded up your mind about them.

Thoughts like this cause us to profile people more and more, which can create barriers between the community and the police and chances to build a repore over time. Every person has a dual personality. We see the impression a person gives and try to form our own opinions without coming to know the person. Don't forget that there is another part to the persons personalit as well that has an entirely different side.

Shift Your View

Empathy is defined as putting yourself in another person's shoes and seeing things from their prospective. When communicating with the public think about how it would feel to be in their shoes and speaking with the police while trying to explain your side of the situation. How would you feel if you had to communicate with someone that did not value what you were saying.

Shifting how you view others does not mean that you have to entirely give up your opinions and what you think. It involves taking a few minutes to stop and reflect on the actions and words of the other person and picturing yourself in their situation. Think about what it would be like to stand in their shoes, being confronted by people with guns, having the ability to take you to jail or end your life. By doing this, we can better understand why they may act or speak a certain way and what can drive them to do what they do. By showing empathy, you are able to connect with this person and create an important relationship to have in your district/ sector.

Don't Show Fake Emotions

In social situations it is never a good idea to fake our emotions or how we feel toward others.

Of course, this does not mean we have full permission to usurp our authority and start ripping them to shreds if we didn't like their ethic back ground. But if you aren't entirely happy about the district you work are care because of a certain group of people living in that district or feel anxious about your surroundings, it is not a good idea to fake a smile or laugh just to appear happy. Remember just be professional.

Faking emotions will more than likely be detected, which can offend others around you or even make them feel insecure. Instead, be honest about how you feel and show honest concern for the people in the district. If the situations warrant be tactful when making an initial contact and offer helpful suggestions for improvement or changes. Although they may not accept your true feelings at first, and may even seem angry about it, in the end they will appreciate the fact that you were honest with them and didn't show a mask of fake emotions with them.

Case Study

Officer Donald realized he was not connecting well with the people living in his district/Sector. Some of of the people were upset with his communication style. They thought he was brash and overbearing, so he thought this would be a good time to show empathy and connect with some of them. He approached Bradly and asked him how he felt about the 9 PM curfew at the basketball court. Donald listened as Bradly expressed anger about it and ranted about the time the park closed. Although Donald thought he may have been over-reacting, he didn't mention these feelings out loud because he didn't want to judge Bradly. Then Officer Donald genuinely told him how he could see his point and he was sorry the park closed at 9 PM. Bradly thanked him for validating his feelings.

Module Four: Active Listening

The average person can speak about hundred and 50 words per minute but I can think alot faster, between 450 600 words a minute. Obviously there is room to multitask in your mind, called listening.

For example, while you are speaking with a victim of A crime, this abundance of nonstop thinking maybe going through your mind:

What am I going to have for lunch?

Should I buy that new motorcycle now or wait till the end of the month?

wonder who was going to get the promotion to Sergeant. What can I do to get off from work earlier today..

See if any of these barriers to active listening happen for you. Check the ones that affect you and start changing them today.

Rehearsing a response: all of your thoughts are putting together a response to the questions that might come up. Are you practicing on what you're going to say.

False reassurances: you, not your head are say yeah, while looking for the tiny opening where you can jump in and speak.

Clichés: there are all kinds of clichés such, as "I'm with you" or "I totally understand", when you really aren't or don't.

Misdirected questions: you ask questions that diverge or interrupt the person speaking and fail to really explore what the person is saying.

Daydreaming: your mind is elsewhere, what your next vacation, or playing tennis on the weekend.

Not focusing: You pay attention to something or someone just outside of the conversation, such as the person who just walked by or the conversation on TV about last nights football game.

Selective listening: You only catch a few words every time you listen.

It is not always enough to simply listen to a person and have the sense of 'waiting to speak'. This will give an officer the chance to resolve conflict or make a real connection. By using active listening, will make the officer more capable of learning about the situation and take an active interest in what they have to say and offer. This concept can not only improve the officers overall listening skills, but the officers overall connections with other people as well.

Attunement

Attunement is defined as being aware and responsive to the Community you serve. When developing active listening skills, this tool is used to better connect with the public and become more 'in tune' with what they are saying. Since attunement relies heavily on nonverbal communication (such as body language), it is important to pay attention to the signals that the other person gives off, as well as the ones we use. Key gestures such as smiling, hand gesturing, eye contact and body movement can make or break a connection. When we use these gestures toward the general public, it can make them feel more connected with the officer, allowing the public to build trust and to open up to the officer. These connections can form bonds that can benefit the officer and the community and build networks for the future.

Don't Jump to Conclusions

Thousands of years of history have demonstrated very conclusively that conflict tends to create more conflict. It's a common error to judge a book by it's cover. While patrolling in urban communities you might hear something or witness someone do something and try to jump to a conclusion about it right away. Maybe you didn't like what they said or heard something you didn't think was appropriate, so you reach conclusions about the entire community rather than the individual. But this quick acting judgment can only harm your relationships, forcing you to miss the chance to really listen to someone and bridge a connection. While you may believe you have all the facts and have reached a final decision, always remember there is another side to the bridge and most likely more information to the story.

Even if you do have everything you need, you may still not be able to process his thought in a way that can be productive or even helpful to anyone since it is based on negativity. If a fellow police officer says something that makes you jump to a conclusion, ask them to repeat it or clarify what they said. Then take a few minutes to reflect on what was said or done and take enough time to form a logical conclusion about what was said. Taking a little extra time may seem like a chore at times, this method can save you from jumping to unnecessary conclusions and ruining the chance to build a relationship with another coworker.

Shift Your Focus

Because of their badge some officers think of them self as untouchable. "We take care of our own", is their moto. But when it comes to active listening, the role is often reversed in

order to focus on the other person. In order to actively listen, we must shift the focus from ourselves to the person speaking at the time and become attune to what they are saying. Steps should include.

1. Turning to face the person

2. Making eye contact with them.

3. During the conversation, nod your head periodically and give them time to pause or rest before jumping into the conversation.

Once they have finished, stay focused on what they're saying. Don't be afraid to ask them to clarify something you didn't hear or something you may have missed. By shifting your focus to them instead of on your thoughts, you should be able to remember and comprehend most of what was said. From here you will be able to offer suggestions or opinions and engage in open conversation with the person. They'll be more likely to openly share with you if they feel as though you honestly are concerned with their problem.

Don't Discount Feelings

One of the biggest faults many police officers have is poor communication in their sectors they patrol.

When we get some bad news or information about a bad situation, we often try to follow it up with "It's not so bad" or "It could be worse". While this may seem like a helpful gesture, it can actually cause more damage than good because it makes the other person feel as though their feelings about the situation are invalid.

It gives the impression that you are not necessarily listening to the problem, but imply trying to brush it over and discount their feelings altogether. When a person is speaking about something they feel strongly about, whether it is about work or personal situations, it is important to recognize that it is the way they feel and that they are entitled to feel that way. Instead of trying to smooth the problem over, listen to what the person is saying and how they are feeling and offer support. Let them know you are there to help and can always lend an ear. They will appreciate the gesture much more than any half-hearted solution or smooth-over phrase.

Case Study

Judy was talking with a coworker of hers about the new computers in the patrol cars. Cindy complained a lot about having to learn how to work the software and how to use it every day. Judy could see where she was coming from, since it frustrated her too. Judy told her that the new computer wasn't so bad, which didn't make Cindy feel any better. But the way Cindy complained, Judy got the impression that she no longer wanted to be a police officer, which made Judy feel upset. But Judy decided to just ask Cindy if that is how she really felt. Cindy says she doesn't dislike the new computer to much to leave, but it does make her very frustrated. Judy was relieved to hear that her friend didn't want to leave and was glad she took the time to listen to Cindy's opinions before making any conclusions.

# Module Five: Insight on Behavior; The warrior mentality

Behavior can be a complicated concept to understand. The best predictor for future behavior is past behavior.

Perception

Perception can be a hard aspect to learn from since most of the time our perception can only be drawn from our own experiences – and we're pretty biased when it come to our own thoughts. Perception is an important tool in controlling behavior because it helps us determine how we can appear to others and how other people's behaviors can influence us. Your belief in yourself can affect your perception and can in turn affect your outward behavior.

We may not always know exactly how people perceive us since many will not say these things out loud, but we can make our own conclusions based on our perception of their behavior.

Do they come close when they speak to you or do they try to move away?

Do they smile and interact with you or do they seem withdrawn?

Do you use these thoughts when you perceive people and their behaviors? It is likely you form some of the same conclusions and determine how to respond to the behaviors they are displaying.

The problem is, training police officers to think like warriors effectively alienates them from the communities they are sworn to protect. **It can also lead them to perceive threats where none exist, escalating what should be minor conflicts into deadly force encounters.** Along with a host of other policies that the criminal justice system has inflicted disproportionately on communities of color—stop and frisk, broken windows, three strikes—police shootings have fostered an atmosphere of deep distrust. Once cops started thinking like **occupying troops,** a clash like the one that followed the killing of Michael Brown in Ferguson, Missouri, became all but inevitable.

"That's the whole idea of the 'thin blue line.' It's the thing that separates society from chaos, but also separates cops from society."

According to the Police Executive Research Forum, a law enforcement think tank, police recruits receive an average of 107 hours of training in firearms and defensive techniques, but only 16 hours in crisis intervention and de-escalating conflicts.

Facts vs. Emotions

The main difference between facts and emotions is that facts are based on definite results while emotions are often involuntary and one-sided. But both facts and emotions can affect our behaviors and change how we act towards others. Facts can drive a conversation and allow people to connect on a logical level. Emotions are involved in everything we do, but sometimes they can affect the impact of our behavior and the information we are talking about.

Any social situation is most likely driven with emotions, and sometimes this can cause facts to become irrelevant and even misconstrue the information given. For example, a male speaker may not be taken seriously at a feminism rally, or a group full of teachers may not listen to a group of school board members. When you recognize that emotion may be driving the situation, it's time to reflect back on the situation and rediscover the facts and figures of the information. You may have to be a leader in the group and remind everyone to focus on the facts and save the emotions for later.

Give me an example of a time when you were very frustrated with a complaint or perpetrator. What did you say or do?

What matters did you used to control yourself are keep yourself poised.

On a scale of one to 10, with 10 being the highest form of control. How effective are you at managing your emotions.

What triggers you, are pushes your buttons the most with perpetrators.

Give me an example of a time you had to totally change or adapt a new strategy and working with someone. What did you do or say?

What do you find to be the hardest part in dealing with change.

On a scale of one to 10, How adaptable are you? What else could you do to improve.

Listen and Watch More

One of the best ways to monitor your behavior and the behavior of others is to learn to listen and watch more than you participate. When listening to others talk, focus on their words, not necessarily the person saying them. Don't get caught up in one or two things they say and try to stay focused on the topic at hand. Even though you want to chime in, avoid making your own predictions and assumptions and continue to listen until the end. By watching and listening more, we are able to better monitor the behaviors of other as well as our own since we are not focused mainly on ourselves. By focusing on the other person and their actions, we can develop better listening skills and catch more information than if we tried to assume it all ourselves.

Tips for better listening:

- Listen for verbal cues
- Watch for nonverbal cues
- Focus on what is being said, not the person
- Be aware of your own behaviors and reactions

Case Study

Robert was meeting with his partner, Rick for lunch to discuss a recent case. When Rick arrived, he seemed agitated and it made Robert feel tenser. Robert noticed that Rick's behavior was making him feel uneasy and wasn't sure how to perceive them. As they talked about the case, Robert noticed Rick's behavior began to shift and he began to ease up. Finally, Robert asked him if something was wrong. It turns out that Rick was having personal trouble at home and it was affecting his work, so he hadn't quite gotten out of his bad mood. Robert offered his support and told Rick he can help him with the work load. Robert was glad he asked Rick about his behavior instead of just focusing on his emotions and feelings about it.

Module Six: Communication

Sadly, talking and listening has often been seen as a tool for simply communicating with other people, but not for building connections and networks. This assumption doesn't recognize the fact that interpersonal communication is a great tool to connect with people on a deeper level and form a connection with them. Speaking interpersonally allows both parties to feel more at ease and open up to one another. Just remember to be an active listener and watch your own body language.

Give Respect and Trust

It is a common courtesy in any conversation to treat the other person respectfully and professionally. By treating their ideas and opinions respectfully and with due consideration, you are showing respect by hearing them out, listening to them, and considering what they have to say with an open mind. When communicating with coworkers, it is important to build rapport and trust by speaking with each other respectfully and giving each other your full attention. After all, they deserved to be treated with dignity and courtesy for their thoughts and opinions. In addition, give your trust to them and let them know that you feel confident enough to speak with them openly. The motions and feelings we put out into the world will come back to us, so don't be afraid to speak openly with your coworkers. They will be impressed that you can give respect and trust so freely and appreciate the effort you are trying to make with them.

Be Consistent

Consistency is a key factor that builds interpersonal relationships. Being consistent in what we say and do shows knowledge and reliability because it helps build a familiar base to start from. People will want to communicate with you because you will become a factor they know they can trust and depend on. In addition, ensure that your actions are consistent with what you say – in other words– do what you say you'll do. If you say you will meet someone after lunch to review a report, ensure that you are there early to greet them. If you volunteered to give a speech at the next work convention, be prepared ahead of time and be ready when the day arrives. Showing you are consistent in turn shows how reliable you are and what an asset you can be for the police department.

Take a few minutes to reflect back on your actions and note if they have been consistent over time. Are there behaviors you can change? What can you do differently in the future?

Always Keep Your Cool

Keeping our cool in tight or stressful situations can be tough and takes a lot of skill to make it through gracefully. It is perfectly normal to feel embarrassed or hurt when someone does something you don't like, such as speaking rudely to you or pointing out a mistake you made. Our first instinct is to possibly lash out at them or try to retaliate by hurting them in return. But the key to strong and professional communication is to keep your cool at all times and not let the negative feelings take over. When something happens that may send you over the edge, take a minute to reflect on what was said and what happened. If needed, you should step back for a few feet to compose yourself. Don't deny the other person their opinion, but let them know how you feel and how it affects you. Kinder coworkers will back track their statements and try to address the problem in less negative terms. If the coworker is unwilling to give respect, realize that their opinion may not be worth the fight.

Tips for keeping your cool:

- Try not to take words personally
- Stop and reflect *what* was said, not *how* it was said
- Make a note to learn from this experience
- Ask yourself if the person had reason for what was said – if so, what can you do to change it?

Observing Body Language

Body language can speak volumes between people, even if it does not have words to accompany it. Many times people may say one message, but their body language can say another, meaning they may not be truthful in what they say. By observing and becoming more aware of body language and what it might mean, we can learn to read people more easily and understand some of their body movements. By better understanding their movements, you can be better prepared to communicate with them, while at the same time better understanding the body language you may be conveying to them. Even though there are times that we can send mixed messages, we can try to get our point across using certain behaviors. Our body language affects how we act with others and how we react to them, as well as how they can react to ours.

Case Study

Danielle was giving a presentation on safety in front of her supervisors and was a little nervous about what they would think. She was friendly with all of them, but was unsure how they would react to her work. During the presentation, she spoke with each supervisor and answered their questions respectfully. As she looked around the room, she didn't see a lot of negative body language, such as yawning or wandering eyes, which she took as a good sign. When her presentation was complete, she spoke with each supervisor and got their opinions and thoughts. One supervisor in particular told Danielle that she didn't like the presentation at all and thought Danielle needed to work harder on the next one. Danielle became furious at her negativity, but took a minute to think it over. She knew it was her supervisor's opinion, and didn't want to let it ruin all her work. She thanked the woman for her insight and told her she would do her best.

Module Seven: Social Cues (I)

Social cues are verbal or non-verbal hints that let us know what someone maybe thinking or feeling. When in a social situation, it is important to keep an eye out for these social cues and ensure our behavior isn't contributing to them. While some cues can be obvious, other may be very subtle, so we must train ourselves to be able to recognize them when they do appear.

Recognize Social Situations

Social situations are not a 'one size fits all' situation. Because the people in each cultural or ethic group are different, we must learn to adapt ourselves to these ever-changing groups – and know how to handle them. This does not mean we have to change who we are or hide our own personality, but rather we can change how we present ourselves around other people. Some of the best hints we can use are the ones we get from other people around us.

How are they behaving?

How are they 'working through' the event?

Do you know all of them?

Are there faces you do not recognize?

With this information in mind, determine what type of social situation you may be in. Is this a formal gathering?

Is it a gang affiliation setting or just a group of coworkers getting together?

Maybe a few friends catching a bite to eat?

The key is to recognize your surroundings and the people involved to help determine how to present yourself.

Questions to ask in a social situation:

- "What is the gathering for?"
- "Who is present?"
- "Do we share common interests?"

The current debate over police reform is often presented as a false choice between two straw men: the aggressive, trigger-happy warrior versus the gentle guardian who thinks he can magically de-escalate every situation. It's not useful to frame the debate exclusively in terms of use of force, because all police officers use force.

A guardian's response to an armed robbery will be no different from a warrior's. What truly matters is the set of principles that guides an officer's actions, whether it's a traffic stop or a school shooting.

The guardian model is premised on cooperation and "protecting civilians from unnecessary indignity and harm," says Stoughton. The warrior model is based on principles of compliance and control, which puts police in an adversarial relationship with the public. It's the cop who threatens to use force on anyone who doesn't follow his orders. Not only is such behavior alienating and provocative, it's just bad policing.

Police officers treating criminals like human beings instead of enemy combatants just seems like common sense.

<u>**It's all in how you talk to people. You've got to show them respect.**</u>

You can't be a wise guy:

'Well, I'm the police!'

It ain't gonna work, because you're making them hostile.

Most situations officers face on a daily basis <u>**don't call for warrior skills**</u>. Their default mode should therefore be guardian-like, and warrior-like only when necessary. But right now the polarities are reversed, and changing that will require an overhaul of police culture no less profound than the one that gave rise to the warrior cop.

Stoughton:

The Eyes Have It

Not all cues from others can be seen right and may be well hidden, but the eyes will always give them away. Without blatantly staring at a person (of course), try to observe how they are looking at you and others. Do certain words or phrases make them blink more or dart their eyes in another direction? Are they staying focused on a subject for a long period of time? Unfortunately, the eyes cannot lie – often. Many feelings or behaviors we try to hide in ourselves will often be shown through the eyes. Common eye behaviors such as rolling the eyes or looking around frequently can be signs of boredom or discomfort. If a person looks at you while talking or moves their eyebrows while listening to you talk, this can be a sign of interest or curiosity. But since these feelings may not be said out loud, or even gestured, it is a key tool to remember when gauging the people around you.

Common eye behaviors:

- Eye rolling
- Blinking too much or too little
- Wandering eyes; not looking directly at a person
- Long blinks

Non-Verbal Cues

It has been said that non-verbal communication is the most powerful form of communication since it can expand beyond voice, tone, and even words. It accounts for over 90% of our communication methods. Although the differences in non-verbal communication can be different in certain situations (amount of personal space or use of hand gestures), most cues can send the same message across the board. Nonverbal cues can include facial expressions, body movements, eye movement, and various gestures and usually are not associated with supported words or phrases. Common non-verbal cues include folding the arms, gripping or moving hands while speaking, rolling the eyes and even misusing the tone of voice. Do you notice these gestures when speaking with people around you? When thinking of your behavior, do you find yourself making any of these gestures when you are in a social situation? If so, think of ways you can try to eliminate some of them and replace them with more welcoming or outgoing gestures instead.

Common non-verbal cues:

- Folding the arms
- Looking around frequently
- Tapping the feet or clasping hands
- Fidgeting
- Moving closer/farther away
-
-

Verbal Cues

Verbal cues are cues that we are more likely to pick up on and notice right away. They are usually done with some sort of emphasis or tone that causes an effect within us, and is mostly likely to stick with us in the future. Phrases such as "Did you see the new *rules* in the handbook?" or "I *can't* wait to see the projections for this week" add emphasis to certain words to stress a point or effect. Other verbal cues can include appropriate pauses when speaking, pitch, or volume of the voice or even speaking too slowly or quickly. These are cues that we can control and use with our voices (hence the term *verbal*) to get a message across. When in a social situation, listen to those around you and determine what verbal cues you can pick up on. Do they sound positive or negative? Do they appropriately portray the message being sent? Do you find yourself using these verbal cues on others? Maybe you emphasized the wrong word or spoke in a higher pitch when trying to speak with a group of people. When we can recognize these cues in others and learn to adapt ourselves to them, we can learn to identify them in ourselves and ensure that we are not putting the wrong message out there.

Common verbal cues:

- Voice tone or pitch
- Word emphasis
- Volume
- Uncomfortable pauses or word inserts

Case Study

Mary was at a small office party the company was holding to discuss new department assignments. She walked around and spoke to all of the employees and chatted with them about work and non-work aspects of their life. She noticed many of them seemed uneasy, since they would avert their eyes or stay away from some of the other workers. Others seemed to be at ease with the changes, since they were openly asking questions and making positive comments. Mary decided to ask one of the workers how they were handling the changes, and although they said it was alright, Mary could tell in their eyes that they were uneasy. She asked them if there was something she could do, but the employee just shook his head. Mary was uncertain if he was really alright, but she supposed she would have to wait and see if he opened up to her or not.

Module Eight: Social Cues (II)

Social cues can often enhance, or even downplay, what is being said or portrayed in a situation. But the social cue needs to be interpreted in the right manner for it to better a social situation – not make it worse. People who are better equipped to identify and understand these social cues are more likely to act appropriately to them, and will be better prepared to respond to them and adapt their behavior.

Spectrum of Cues

As in all situations, there is always a possibility for going to one extreme to the other without having any middle ground in between. For social cues, it can be a fairly wide spectrum with plenty of variations. On one side of the spectrum, a person can be very obvious with their cues, such as speaking very loudly or making very large and awkward hand gestures. These types of cues are easy to spot and can often make people feel uncomfortable right away. On the other hand, there are cues that are more subtle and can often be missed if not recognized right away, such as excessive eye blinking or adding a tone to their words.

Unfortunately, these types of cues may go unnoticed and can portray the wrong message when they may not be intended to. They key point is being able to recognize each side of this spectrum and the different ways a social cue can go wrong and right at the same time. When you learn the extremes they can reach, you're better equipped to catch the cues in between and adapt your behavior faster.

Review and Reflect

It's a natural behavior to want to react to a cue we may recognize and want to confront right away. Are you bored? Did I offend you? Did you understand? But these approaches are not the best solution to connect with people and better understand their behavior. When you notice a social cue, such as someone rolling their eyes or speaking in a shrill voice at you, take a moment to stop and review the action. Take notice if it is being directed at you or if others around you are subject to it as well. Does the behavior continue? Maybe the behavior was a onetime occurrence?

Reflect on what you can do to adapt yourself to the situation. Was there something you said to trigger this feeling? Does this person have something they want to share? Or maybe you just need to take a step back from this person. Sometimes they need a moment to review and reflect as well, and may need some personal space to do it. Whatever your results, remember to refrain from jumping to conclusions about the cues we encounter. Always take a minute to two before responding with your own actions.

Being Adaptable and Flexible

"Tactical pause."

Even though there are times we can pick up on these social cues, we may be able to change them or even get away from them as soon as we'd like. These are the times we must learn to be flexible and adapt to the situation. We all know that not all situations will be comfortable for us and we may need to find a way to adapt until it's over. Sometimes the room can have more people than we are comfortable with or maybe the other visitors are sending cues of boredom or annoyance, but don't let these cues sink you. Be flexible to the group and reflect on what you can do to help the situation. Try to start a conversation with people that seem distant or unsure. Lead by example and speak in lower pitches or in casual tones. Many times the people around you will catch onto the cues you are sending out and will become adaptable as well. This great trick doesn't always work in all situations, but it is one way we can help ourselves adapt and manage through a difficult situation.

But cops *are* playing by the rules—rules that favor them. Between 2004 and 2011, according to an analysis by The *Wall Street Journal*, officers were cleared of wrong doing in more than 99 percent of fatal shootings. The problem isn't that the shootings might have been legally justified—the problem is that they were often unnecessary.

Personal Space

Edward Hall was one of the first people to define and characterize the space around us – our different level of spaces. The outer most space around us is our public space, such as in a large room. Coming in closer is our social space, such as talking with a group of friends. The next inward space is our personal space, which is usually within arms' reach of us. This space is usually on reserve for 'invitation-only', meaning we do not like for people to be in our personal space unless we initiate it and welcome them over.

In social situations, this can be a hard thing to maintain. The key is to refrain from being rude to someone who may have encroached on your space. If this person is too close, take a few steps to the side instead of backwards, which creates subtle distance and doesn't appear as though you are backing away. If you must leave a group of people, or even just one, that are too close, always excuse yourself politely and move to an open area. If possible, take a few steps around the room every so often, which keeps you mobile and doesn't allow for crowding. Remember, this is the time to be adaptable, so you may need to be flexible with your surroundings to feel more at ease.

Tips for keeping your personal space personal:

- Excuse yourself politely when leaving a group
- Step to the side a step or two to create subtle distance
- Walk often or roam about the area – if possible
- Opt for a handshake when greeting people – it allows for the other person to stay at arm's length
- Be aware of cultural differences in personal space

Case Study

Andrew was working with a group of coworkers that was developing a new project. Many of them worked on different shifts, so it was hard for them to keep their schedules together. Right away Andrew noticed many of them displayed very different social cues, such as being very aggressive and some were more nonverbal. As he reviewed the situation, he realized that if he was going to work well with the group, he would need to adapt some of his habits and attitudes. So Andrew made sure he kept his mind open and made himself flexible in order to get the project finished. He stayed out of everyone's personal space, but was available when needed. At the end of the project, Andrew reflected back on his experience and noted that even though it helped him learn new social cues, it was not something he thought he could get used to.

 Unlike soldiers, police officers mission is to avoid killing. "Our strength comes from that, our purity comes from that,". "We must never fail to communicate that message. That's what the guardian model is about. Treating people with dignity, without a doubt, is at the foundation of what we have to do. That's what they lost track of in Ferguson."

Module Nine: Conversation Skills

Conversation is like an adhesive that can bring people together. It can make friends, create networks, and even seal a deal. But it can have the opposite effect when used in the wrong way. Some key points about holding a conversation include the topic, the tone, and even presentation. Only you are familiar with how to work on these aspects, conversation in social situations will become second nature.

Current Events

Discussing current events can be a great skill to build conversation and become engaged in the real world around us. Tragic current events, such as war or weather disasters, can bring in many members to a conversation and can share empathy and sorrow among people. Of course more pleasant events, such as economic upswing and the cost of gas going down can be a more uplifting line of topics to discuss and create a lighter atmosphere. Discussing what is going on in the world allows for group members to connect on many levels. After all, we live here and we see what's going on! But be aware of current events that can cross into sensitive topics such as politics or religion, since these can offend some people and cause tension among a group.

Conversation Topics

Sometimes when we speak among other people in social situations, the lines of safe conversation topics can become blurry. We can become too comfortable and begin talking about subjects that can seem fine to some people, but can be offensive or rude to others. It is usually recommended to stick with topics that are considered 'safe' for everyone, such as common work areas or hobbies. Some other safe topics include sporting events, television or movies and even forms of travel. These can help people connections and friendships without crossing into dangerous territories. Some infamous topics to avoid include religion, gossip, risqué jokes, and the government/politics, since these can cause tension and arguments among group members, even if it was not the intention.

If all else fails, you can always talk about the weather!

Topics to avoid in a group:

- Religion

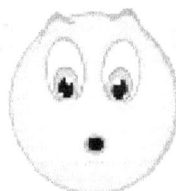

- Politics

- Personal health

- Prejudice topics (racism, sexism, etc.), including jokes

Cues to Watch For

As we've come to learn, we're not psychic and can't always predict what other people are thinking. This is why it is important to learn about verbal and nonverbal cues to look and listen for when in a social situation. Remember the nonverbal cues such as crossing the arms or turning their heads away to signal signs of discomfort or disinterest. These can be signs to change the current subject or recognize that something inappropriate was probably said. However, cues such as full smiles or open hands can be positive in nature and can signal approval and happiness.

Many cues that are given are from the subconscious are not always shared on purpose, especially if some feels offended or angry, in which they may not want to express out loud. So while in the midst of a conversation, look around at the people talking and the people listening. Do you see any of the typical cues, such as eye rolling, loud speaking, turned away bodies or inappropriate laughter? If so, what can you do to change the situation or even adapt yourself to it?

Cues to keep an eye out for:

- Cues signaling boredom or annoyance
- Cues signaling anger or offense
- Cues signaling different types of body language – whether open or closed
- Cues signaling for interest or comfort

Give People Your Attention

Whether you're in a conversation with just one person, a few people, or even a large group, it is important for you to give them your attention. It shows your respect for the person, or  people, talking and that you really value what they are saying. When listening to other people, nod your head and make eye contact with them to let them know they have your attention and that you are listening. This can make people feel more at ease with you and make them not only put their trust in you, but feel more confident when speaking with you. If you know a head of time that you will be in a group or be speaking with others, remember to turn off your phone or set it to vibrate, so it will not be a distraction. The emails or notices can usually wait until after your conversation.

Tips to remember:

- Make eye contact
- Nod and show facial movements
- Ask questions or make a follow up comment
- Remove distractions, such as cell phones

Case Study

Tina was having a group discussion with some of her coworkers during one of their weekly meetings. One of the topics that came up was about the government and the effect it had on the company. While Tina thought this would be interesting to discuss, she thought that the mention of government and politics at work could start arguments between coworkers. So Tina decided to change the subject to the recent growth of the company and how it was doing so well with the new changes. She noticed some of the other coworkers let out a small sigh, possibly out of relief. Soon they were discussing current events, which made everyone feel more connected. As each person spoke, Tina made sure to offer her full attention to let them know she was interested in what they had to say. Soon the group was talking about much more positive topics that were 'safer' to discuss at work.

Module Ten: Body Language

Body language is a form of language that relies on body movements as gestures. It accounts for over 90% of the language we use in society – the other 10% consisting of actual words or phrases. It can provide cues and hints about how the other person is feeling and thinking. Learning to read body language is an important lesson to know since people may not always simply say what is on their mind, but will definitely show it in their movements.

Be Aware of Your Movements

Unless the room is covered in mirrors, we may not always be aware of the body language we are displaying to people around us. Since the majority of body language is nonverbal, we cannot always control what we show and what we are 'saying', so we must learn to be aware of our own movements and gestures to prevent any miscommunications. Some tips to try out on your own are to look at yourself in a reflective surface, such as a mirror or a piece of glass, and practice saying things from a conversation. Do you show any signs of body language – and what are they? When in the room, listen to what other people are saying when they talk to you. Don't put up defense barriers and block them out. Look at the way they act or behave when they are around you or speak directly to you. Their body language can often let you know how you are coming across and let you know what you may be putting out into the room, even if you are not aware of it.

It's Not What You Say – It's How You Say It

When we rely on our words alone and open our mouths to let them out, we can accidentally let fly all sorts of meanings and phrases that were never meant to come out. Linguistic tools such as tone, emphasis, and even pitch can make even the simplest or nicest phrase come out very wrong. When we speak, the emphasis on certain words comes naturally, which can seem off-putting to others and can lead to a confused message. It can often lead them to question if that is what you meant to say or if you just didn't know what you were trying to say to begin with.

Practice saying the following phrase with tone and emphasis on a different word each time:

- "*I'd* like to help you with your situation."
- "I'd like to help you *with* your situation."
- "I'd like to help you with your *situation*."

Do you hear the different messages that the same phrase can have with different words stressed and tones implied? The words we say only make up half of our message – the rest is in how you say it.

It's all in how you talk to people. You've got to show them respect.

Open vs. Closed Body Language

Our body language can be like a traffic light to the people around us. Open body language can signal a green light for people to approach you and engage in conversations with you. However, closed body language can signal a red light and make people want to keep their distance from you while they can. Open body language includes gestures such as having open hands and palms, making eye contact, and reaching out to greet someone. This can also you seem more persuasive when speaking with other people and gain their trust. Closed body language such as crossing the arms, turning the head away and constantly fidgeting are much less inviting, and will not get other people to come around. This kind of body language can make you seem defensive and withholding from those around you. If you wish to communicate well with others, it is important to realize how to use (and not use) your body to speak out.

Example of open body language:

- Feet facing forward
- Smiling face
- Open palms
- Making eye contact

Examples of closed body language:

Looking away or around the room

Crossing the arms or legs

Turning your body away

Rolling the eyes or blinking excessively

Communicate with Power

Effective communication is key in any situation. When you communicate with others, you want it to be a powerful message that they will take away with them when you part ways. No one wants their message to come across as week and easily forgotten. Before you even begin to form words, think about what you want to say, and how you want your message to come across. Make notes of any wrongful tones or emphasis might be used and prevent it. When you are done speaking, listen to what the other person has to say and show signs of active listening, such as nodding your head or asking follow up questions. Turn your body to the other person and give them your full attention during the session. As always, remove any distractions that can incur the wrong body language, such as checking a ringing phone or being distracted while checking emails.

Tips for communicating with power:

- Think before you speak
- Be an active listener
- Watch for verbal and nonverbal cues
- Be aware of your body language

Case Study

Seth was speaking with a couple of his coworkers about the recent report they had finished. It was a challenging report, so some of the coworkers were still tense. When Seth approached them, they would cross their arms or turn their body away from him. He thought maybe he was coming across as too aggressive in his movements, so he decided to try and make softer, more open movements. Some of them felt more at ease, but others did not. They were not happy about how Seth had given the results of the report and had implied that they had not worked hard enough. Seth then realized that the words he had used during their discussion must have come across wrong and he needed to readdress to topic. So Seth gathered everyone together and re-discussed the report, this time making sure to be aware of not only the words he used, but the tone and emphasis as well.

Module Eleven: Building Rapport

Rapport is used in the business world to build professional relationships and networks. It helps  gain confidence and trust in other people and makes them feel more at ease. When in social situations, this can include simple techniques such as mirroring and sharing common interests. Building rapport early on can help you be successful later in business and create less awkward moments in social situations.

Take the High Road

 Building rapport is about standing out and standing above others around you to make connections and networks with various people. While this can seem like an aggressive gesture, it is actually just the opposite. Taking the high road is being humble and putting others before yourself. Don't treat the situation like a competition, but rather more of a showcase. Show others that you can be a great listener as well as a contributor to a team or group. While others are scrambling around you to show off their talents and skills to come out as the 'top dog', take the road less taken and have a lower profile to display. Offer your input and take interest in what the other person is saying. By showing you can stand out over the others without trying to crush them shows that you can display great skills without having to put others down in the process, which benefits the entire group. Remember, building rapport is about building connections- not destroying them.

Forget About Yourself

When you want to build rapport with another person, or group, the key element is to actually take yourself out of the equation. Although you have things to say and contribute, spend more time listening to what they have to say and ask follow up questions to expand on their ideas. Yes, you know you have great opinions and ideas and want to share them with the world, but this is not the time. Building rapport requires you to develop an honest interest in another party besides yourself. Become interested in the people around you and what they do and stand for. When people feel that you care about their lives and what they do, they are more inclined to open up and share more, opening the gates to build stronger connections and longer relationships.

Key points to remember:

- Be an active listener
- Show interest in their ideas and thoughts
- Ask for follow up information
- Offer opinions as needed, but focus on them

Remembering People

When we meet new people, sometimes the names or faces can become a blur. Most people are great at remembering one or the other, but rarely both. But rapport depends on being able to recall a person at a later time over many encounters. One of the main reasons we forget a person's name or face is because we are not truly listening or paying attention when we are being introduced. Don't be nervous and put your mind at ease so that you can easily register the person's face and hearing their name with it. When you look at the person, look for any features that stand out, such as hair color, facial features, scars or even the use of make-up. Remembering a key characteristic while fully listening to their name will help keep them associated in your brain to retrieve at a later date when needed.

Tips to remember name and faces:

- Say their name immediately after hearing it
- Don't be afraid to ask them to repeat their name
- Associate a gesture with their greeting, such as a handshake or smile
- Remember distinct features

Ask Good Questions

You cannot expect to get anywhere with people if you do not know more about them and form a connection with them. One of the best ways to start building this connection is to ask good questions that allow them to share their pearls of wisdom and what they have come to know over time. In turn, they will usually ask for your opinions or thoughts after they have shared, pulling you into to create a network of ideas. The key is asking questions about them and their company, which gives them plenty of area to talk about themselves. Ask open-ended questions that pertain to what they do or don't like about their area and what kind of advice they would offer newcomers. Try to avoid simple yes or no questions, or questions that can make you seem as though you are encroaching on their territory. You're trying to build a bridge between people, not burning it behind you.

Sample questions to ask:

- "What do you enjoy most about _____?"
- "What kind of advice would you offer someone like me?"
- "What are some of your accomplishments with the company?"
- "What is one thing you would want everyone to know about your business?"

Case Study

Ellen was a new employee to a group of marketers. She was fairly shy to speak with them, but wanted to build rapport and gain associates while she was here. To begin with, as she met each one of her coworkers, she made an effort to remember their names and faces for future reference. She made sure she let them know she was available to help when needed and could help out with different tasks. While Ellen still remembered to do her share of the work, she tried to think more about her coworkers and focused less on herself so that she could get to know everyone better. When she did get a chance to speak with them, she always asked in depth questions and asked for their advice. Over time, Ellen had built a great rapport with this group of coworkers and felt like she had built a great network with them as well.

References

Dr. Donald W. Slowik, upset citizens and customer service, how to deal with the angry, difficult, demanding public the Evergreen press 1998 second edition.

Lisa Ford, David McNair, and William Perry Exceptional customer service, published by Adams business 2009.

Henry M. Jensen Kraemer Junior, from values to action, the four principles of values-based leadership. Josie Bass publishing 2011.

Renée Evenson, customer service training 101 second edition 2011.

Bruce W. McLendon, customer service and local government planners press American planning Association. 1992.

Daniel Goleman, emotional intelligence why it can matter more than IQ. 1994.

Moshe Zeidner, Gerald Matthews, and Richard D. Roberts, what we know about emotional intelligence, how it affects learning, work, relationships, and are mental health. 2009.

Jeanne Siegel, PhD, the five essential tools for building powerful and effective relationships, the language of emotional intelligence. 2008.

Emmett C. Murphy, Mark A. Murphy, leading on the ads of chaos. The 10 critical elements for success in volatile times. Prentice-Hall press. 2002.

John C. Maxwell, there is no such thing as business ethics, published by Warner books, 2003

Richer a. Howard, Clinton D.Korver ethics (for the real world), creating a personal code to guide decisions in work and life, Harbor business press Boston Massachusetts 2008.

Joshua Halberstam every day ethics, inspire solutions to real-life dilemmas, published by Penguin group 1993.

Robert Wandberg, PhD, ethics, doing the right thing, Press 2001.

William D Hitt, ethics and leadership putting theory into practice, Battelle press 1990.

Robert K. Cooper, PhD. And Ayman Sawaf, executive EQ, emotional intelligence in leadership and organization. Advanced intelligence technology, LLC 1997

Hendrie Weisinger, PhD, emotional intelligence at work, Jossey Bass 2000.

E. J. Bond, ethics and human well-being Blackwell publishers LTD 1996.

F.

John C. Maxwell ethics 101 when every leader needs to know, Time Warner book group 2003.

Ferguson, career skills library, professional ethics and etiquette third edition, infobase published 2009.

Dennis Collins, a set of business ethics, creating an organization of high integrity and superior performance. John Wiley and Sons Inc. 2009

Adele being. Lynn, the EQ difference, a powerful plan for putting emotional intelligence to work American management Association 2005.

www.ingramcontent.com/pod-product-compliance
Lightning Source LLC
Chambersburg PA
CBHW081153180526
45170CB00006B/2053